RURAL
SURVEILLANCE

A Cop's Guide to Gathering Evidence in Remote Areas

Van Ritch

Paladin Press • Boulder, Colorado

Rural Surveillance:
A Cop's Guide to Gathering Evidence in Remote Areas
by Van Ritch

Copyright © 2003 by Van Ritch

ISBN 13: 978-1-58160-380-4
Printed in the United States of America

Published by Paladin Press, a division of
Paladin Enterprises, Inc.
Gunbarrel Tech Center
7077 Winchester Circle
Boulder, Colorado 80301 USA
+1.303.443.7250

Direct inquiries and/or orders to the above address.

PALADIN, PALADIN PRESS, and the "horse head" design
are trademarks belonging to Paladin Enterprises and
registered in United States Patent and Trademark Office.

Visit our Web site at www.paladin-press.com

Table of Contents

This book is dedicated to the many great men and women who make extraordinary sacrifices to assist their fellow citizens in need—the ones who put themselves at risk in order to get the job done, catch the bad guys, find a missing child, make a case, or find a lost person. They walk among us every day, these "ordinary" people who only want to do what is right and help others. While our population worships its celebrities and idolizes the wealthy, the real heroes in our society go about their business performing remarkable feats and taking incredible risks.

To those exceptional people in the military, law enforcement, fire and rescue teams, and private volunteers that step up to the plate and volunteer when more timid souls turn away, this book is dedicated to you.

Preface

This book was written as a guide to any organization or individual that needs to conduct searches or surveillance in a rural and remote environment. Although it may make for interesting reading to others, it is designed for those who must plan, support, and participate in rural surveillance operations.

A covert rural surveillance operation is not just a simple walk in the woods or a working camping trip; at a minimum it is a risky undertaking. It is something that requires time, effort, support, and most of all, commitment. This commitment must come not only from those on the ground but also from those in direct support of the operation and from the leadership of the organization. It takes a strong, visionary leader to see the value in developing, training, and deploying a rural surveillance team.

The following chapters are not the bits and pieces of nice-to-have information that the author happened to hear or read about in a hunting magazine or a how-to book he came across. They are the result of training and doing it! Many of the lessons and much of the information included in this text is the result of oversights and major screw-ups. Often, the best teacher is making (and luckily surviving) a major mistake, learning from it, and never, ever forgetting it. A lot of that is incorporated in this book.

Having conducted surveillance in both rural and urban environments, I can tell you that there is no comparison. The tactics and skills needed to conduct surveillance in a rural environment go far beyond those that are needed to carry out an operation in an urban setting. (It should be stated that there are situations that can arise during sensitive urban surveillance where the training and skills needed for a rural surveillance can be used with success. I can recall once where the surveillance in a criminal investigation in a large city in Europe succeeded only because we were able to get close enough to the target by using rural surveillance skills.)

Sitting in a surveillance van in a wooded area is not what I would term rural surveillance. Rural surveillance employs the skills of a good surveillance operator plus the attributes and cunning of a tracker scout. It takes a very well-trained and dedicated person to be an effective rural surveillance operator—someone who possesses a unique skill that includes patience, endurance, and courage. Any organization, whether involved in law enforcement or another field, that can develop this capability will be well rewarded as a result of the accomplishments made by a rural surveillance team. This book is written with the intent of assisting the development of that capability.

Chapter One:
Introduction to Rural Surveillance

It was never my intent to write a book about rural surveillance. When I developed the course for law enforcement personnel and investigators it was because I saw a need and realized that even today there remain large rural areas we often cannot adequately police. Looking back, I realize that this book was being put together subconsciously when I was training and doing rural surveillance as I was serving in the U.S. Army. But I believe my first realization of the desperate need for this type of training for law enforcement came as I was watching the evening news.

A small group of men had committed several felonies in a rural area and had shot at members of the local police before retreating into the backwoods. The news carried the story for more than a week, showing how the local sheriff's deputies could only stay with their patrol vehicles and monitor the area at road intersections. During one of the news broadcasts an interview was conducted with law enforcement officials who were asked why they weren't doing more to apprehend the felons. The answer, basically, was that they weren't going to put their officers at risk by going into the area; they didn't have anyone trained to do that type of thing.

Several things immediately struck me about that answer. First, it was the truth; they weren't trained for such an operation. Second, it was a smart and brave decision not to send officers without training into such a situation; they would likely have been injured or killed. And third, this law enforcement agency, like many throughout the country, was not adequately prepared to conduct certain enforcement operations in rural environments.

It also occurred to me that before any law enforcement agency can conduct a SWAT operation, drug raid, or hostage rescue it must collect information about the target. That requires good surveillance, often for days at a time. How many law enforcement agencies or investigators do you know of that can successfully conduct surveillance on a critical target in a rugged rural area? I only know of a few such departments, and only a very few of their officers are trained to successfully conduct such an operation.

Some might say that this type of operation or surveillance is rarely needed. I would respond by saying that it is rare only because departments aren't prepared to carry it out. Hostage negotiations are rare, too, but when they become necessary you'd better be prepared. Conducting covert rural surveillance takes a unique type of law enforcement officer, and doing it for an extended time takes a truly disciplined team of dedicated men. It has been my experience that most law enforcement agencies have officers who are capable in covert rural surveillance operations; the department just hasn't made the commitment to prepare itself for this capability.

What would it take for a department to develop this capability? First, this is not the type of endeavor a department should undertake without a long-term commitment. There isn't a department in the world that can, in reality, buy some equipment, conduct a little training, and say that it has a rural surveillance capability. True rural surveillance capability means that they can observe a target for hours, days, or even weeks without being detected. They can collect enough information to conduct a successful raid or hostage rescue operation. This commitment must come from senior management of a department and it will take courage, because this decision will likely meet with some stiff opposition from those within as well as some outside the department. They might not understand the need and balk at the resources needed to start and sustain such a capability. But in reality, having such a capability would more than pay for itself in the benefits it would bring to the department and to the community it serves.

I am aware of one such instance in which a sheriff made the commitment to have rural surveillance capability and it paid off for both him and the community. Several years ago a family out on a hike realized that their young son was missing. They spent much of the day looking for him but had no luck in finding any sign of the boy. The family finally contacted the sheriff's office for help. Fortunately, the sheriff's office had a team that was exceptionally skilled at tracking and working in the rugged rural environment where the boy was last seen. This team had searched for escaped prisoners in this area in the past and was familiar with the area. More importantly, they were a team and had worked together many times before—this is critical to any group working together in a rural area and it was especially important given the terrain they were working in on this search operation.

In the search for the missing child, the team worked the area long into the night. Sometime after midnight the team leader made the decision to call off the search and continue it in the morning. He made the decision based upon his experience and the knowledge that they would have more success in daylight. The decision proved to be the right one as the child was found alive and well, though cold and exhausted, the next day. He had been hiding from the "strangers" on the team, which experienced searchers know is common in cases of lost, confused, and scared children.

This situation had a happy ending because the sheriff of that county had previously made the right decision to have a team capable of operating in rugged rural terrain. The leader of that team told me that when they found the child he was hiding in an area where volunteers very likely would not have found him.

As an added benefit, the sheriff there was reelected shortly afterward in large part due to the fact that this child was rescued by his team. The same rural surveillance team has also been successful in tracking down escaped convicts when other agencies could not find them and has successfully surveilled numerous targets in their area that might otherwise have gone undetected. Due to the vision of that sheriff, a child is alive, several criminals were quickly apprehended, and at least one jurisdiction has not surrendered its ability to police all of its area.

Today there are more than 3,000 sheriff's offices in the United States. According to the Department of Agriculture, rural America comprises 2,305 counties, contains 83 percent of the nation's landmass, and is home to more than 20 percent of the U.S. population, just over 55 million people. That's a lot of folks and as we have seen in the past few years that is also the opportunity for a lot of crime. Of the 2,305 counties, each of which has a sheriff's office, it would be interesting to know how many of these departments really have the ability to conduct surveillance operations on possible criminal activities taking place in their jurisdictions. I am sure that many of them have several fine and capable officers they could call on to take a look at remote sites, but that is not the same as having a team that can operate for an extended amount of time in a rural area.

Some would argue that having such a team, even a small team, is a waste of precious law enforcement resources. They would say that putting a team together would take away from other duties or those resources that are already stretched to the limit. Nothing could be further from the truth. In fact, developing and

Training officers to perform their duties in rural areas is critical.

maintaining such a capability would mean more bang for the buck and would only add to the department's capabilities. In addition, forming a team with high standards often increases morale and gives others in the department something to strive for. Many of the people who enter law enforcement do so for the challenge and the desire to do something that makes a difference. Having a capable rural surveillance team that trains and operates together would satisfy both needs. It would also send a message to criminals: you are not always going to be able to get away with your crimes just because you choose to operate in the remote areas of the country.

Anyone who follows the trends and studies criminal behavior will tell you that crime has and is continuing to move to the remote areas of the country. No one really knows why this is although there is no shortage of "experts" to

tell us their theories. Let me just pass on to you what a number of deputies and sheriffs who are dealing with this problem every day have told me—it's rising because it's easy, there is less risk, and there isn't much that law enforcement can do to stop it!

The truth of the matter is that more and more people over the past several years have moved back to the rural areas to escape the crime and stress of living in overpopulated urban areas. Ironically, these people end up being just as vulnerable because there is a lower percentage of law enforcement officers in those areas.

Many wealthy families have bought and furnished nice second homes in remote areas of the country. Well, there are a lot of smart criminals, and it hasn't taken them long to figure out that there is very little risk in burgarlizing a well-furnished house that is either unoccupied or in an area with very little law enforcement presence.

As an example of how the lack of rural policing capabilities creates problems, I'll relate a situation that has been going on for some time and still continues today. On the Outer Banks of North Carolina, there are number of resort areas that are heavily populated with vacationers throughout the summer. However, once the summer vacations are over and the kids go back to school, these areas are deserted except for the people who live and work there year-round.

In the past several years this area has become increasingly popular as a place for people in the upper income brackets to build second homes or summer homes. These are not like the old beach houses that still populate much of the area; rather, they are expensive and well-furnished homes that sit unoccupied for much of the year.

In a conversation with the chief of police for one of these areas, he told me how they often had more difficult problems during the off-season, when there were fewer people in the area. When these homes sit empty and there aren't many people around to keep an eye on their neighbors' homes, break-ins get out of control.

If you are familiar with beach areas you know that there are a lot of spots on the beach that have little or no vegetation. However, if you travel inland for a few hundred yards there is often dense vegetation and underbrush. Criminals know they can move from house to house undetected, break into these homes, and steal everything. With a small force and limited resources, the police are ill prepared to deal with this continuous crime.

The police chief is frustrated that one house gets hit several times a year because the thieves know the owner is rarely there. This is a wealthy homeowner with lots of electronics and stereo equipment that he replaces every time they're stolen. The thieves know they can move from one home to the next using the underbrush as cover; if a patrol car happens to cruise the area they simply hide in the brush until the threat has passed.

How could training in rural surveillance help in this situation? I do not think that it could solve the problem; there isn't any one thing that will prevent a thief from stealing when he sees an opportunity as inviting as this situation. However, the police have to do more than just patrol the area and shine a few lights! By training some of the more motivated officers, a department could have a useful additional capability.

I am not advocating that the chief try to have officers, or even one officer, sit on a house all night for several nights to try and catch someone breaking in. He will never have the kind of assets it would take to be able to do that. But having several officers trained to move in thick vegetation at night, able to blend into the area unseen and capable of doing some elementary tracking, might help to catch the thieves. Not only that, but if the word spread that the police were taking a more proactive role, were getting out of their patrol cars and moving through the area, it could have a dramatic effect on the amount of activity taking place in the area. It would also probably do a lot to raise morale within the department.

I never cease to be amazed at what one individual or small group of people can accomplish when they set their minds to it. One sheriff's department in a county near Charlotte, North Carolina, was having a problem with assaults and rapes of high school girls in rural areas where kids would meet with their friends to party. Instead of partying in the same place each time, these kids would get together in different remote or semi-remote areas so they could drink and smoke without getting caught. Unfortunately, this also made it easy for the young women to become victims.

Fortunately, these crimes were occurring in a jurisdiction whose sheriff had the vision to train selected members of his SWAT team in rural surveillance. This team had had several previous successes in using its capability to conduct raids, and the decision was made to put several members in the area where the kids were partying. During the first several outings the team members detected no threats to the kids, but after several surveillances deputies detected a middle-aged man in the area. Later on, one night this man made his way toward the partying kids, but before he could cause any harm he was detained by the officers. An investigation later determined that he was the one who had previously assaulted and raped the young women. He is now a guest of the state prison system.

Could he have been caught eventually by conventional means? Maybe, maybe not. But the fact is that he was apprehended by a group of dedicated and well-trained officers who might not have caught him as soon as they did without this training. Keep in mind that in this situation, like in many others, the team needed to move into the area undetected. They were able to remain undetected by both the people they were looking for and those they were trying to protect.

This team continues to have success as a result of its training. With each operation the team members continue to refine, improve, and expand their rural operation and surveillance capabilities. They truly police their entire jurisdiction. The impact on morale has led to immeasurable benefits both for the team and for the department. In fact, many officers are volunteering for the SWAT team not because they want to do SWAT operations, but because they want to conduct rural surveillance operations. Several members of the team are now also part of the department's investigative unit because of the need within investigations for a rural surveillance capability. Remember that this is a sheriff's department that has a lot of cases to investigate throughout a county that is more than 90 percent rural.

Although rural surveillance has tremendous applications and benefits for a sheriff's office, it by no means is something that is only of benefit to them. Some of the most exciting and risky surveillances I have ever conducted or am aware of have taken place in urban areas, but rural surveillance skills can be applied anywhere the understanding and appreciation for cover and concealment are required.

In one situation, a team I was working with had to surveil a site in a large coastal resort town. There was good information to believe that a dead drop[1] would be used by an individual who was currently under surveillance. We knew the dead drop had been loaded earlier in the day and that the person being watched was periodically moving through the surrounding area to determine if the area or the drop was under surveillance. We also had strong reason to believe that he would either unload the dead drop when it became dark or possibly at first light. This had been his technique in the past, and there was no reason to believe this time would be any different. If we waited until we knew he was heading to the area it would be too late to get into position, so we had to move in long before the subject got there. The dead drop was so well positioned that it was concealed from observation all around by very thick bushes. Although this made it an ideal location for a drop or a short meeting or exchange of contraband, it also allowed us to set up surveillance right on top of the site. Due to the sensitivity of the operation, we had to assume that the subject might have the area under observation to check for any surveillance or other threats prior to entering the area.

We determined that we would need more than one person in the hide site due to the amount of time the operation might take and for safety reasons. Given the nature of the area we also felt that, once in place, the team members in the site might have to remain for more than 24 hours before a second team could replace them. Fortunately, the vegetation was made up of large, thick bushes. The bad part was that it was so thick that getting in took real work. Imagine two grown men turning a corner in a large city park and fighting to get into a group of very dense bushes quickly before anyone else happened by. We had other team members looking out for us but it didn't make getting in there any easier. Having a good, reliable support team is critical to a successful rural surveillance operation, and in following chapters this will be addressed in detail.

Once out of sight, we had to slowly cut away small parts of the underbrush to position ourselves and our equipment for an extended stay. It was critical that anything we cut away could not be detected from the outside of the bushes and would not take away from the cover we were depending on. Once in position, where we could both observe the dead drop without moving, we began our surveillance. After watching the site for the entire night, very early the next morning the suspect finally moved into the area, unloaded the dead drop and left the area. We were able to see him do this and to get photographs of him in the act.

This operation took place more than 10 years ago and used many of the same techniques used to collect information against terrorists in Northern Ireland and other locations around the world. With today's technology it might not always be necessary to go to an extreme such as this, but as many police and lawyers will tell you, nothing is as good as having an eyewitness to back up what the tape recording or photograph reveals. Also, if you are going to take equipment into an area and install it, you'd better have someone putting it in who understands cover and concealment.

The use of rural surveillance requires a high degree of skill and professionalism to ensure the safety and success of the deployed officers, the covert nature of the operation, and the protection of citizens. Rural surveillance has a wide range of applications, and in many respects they are similar to those encountered in conventional surveillance. The primary objective is to obtain intelligence or evidence that may aid in solving a crime, identifying criminal activity, or planning for a raid or rescue operation. Individuals who are properly trained and have proven themselves to be capable of successfully conducting rural surveillance operations usually also prove to be excellent at surveillance operations in an urban environment. This is likely due to the fact that they learn patience and how to observe items in detail.

RURAL CRIME

Although the studies on rural crime and justice are sparse when compared to the volumes written on urban crime, it is evident that rural environments are different from urban areas in ways that affect policing, crime, and public policy. There are reasons today's society needs to pay more attention to policing and rural crime.

- Rural areas are often used to produce drugs, such as marijuana and methamphetamines.
- Rural areas are used as shipment points for illegal drugs, stolen auto parts, and illegal cash.
- Some urban crime networks, such as street gangs, are setting up satellite operations in rural areas.
- Rural areas have special crime problems, such as organized theft of livestock, equipment, and grain. All this is enormously costly for both the victims and society.

Unfortunately, many law enforcement departments in rural areas depend more on pure luck than on having a team of well-trained officers to work the crime. Part of our problem as a society is that we often have difficulty defining "rural." As one sheriff stated, "Rural is like pornography; I can't precisely define it but I know it when I see it." A lot of people throughout the country still believe that a rural area is "where there are a lot of farms." In reality, as a society we have a very unrealistic view of what is rural. Less than 10 percent of the rural labor force is significantly involved in farming, and less than 10 percent of the rural population actually live on farms. This means that many of those living in rural areas work in urban areas, or they may not work at all. Residents may be retirees, which leads to special problems regarding crime. Others may be involved in illegal activities to support themselves.

A rural area may also be defined by its

demographics. In a rural area there are going to be fewer people and they will be more isolated. There is much less human activity than in urban areas and there are fewer roads. These factors all cause unique problems for any type of surveillance operations. In an urban surveillance operation you can blend in with other people and among the traffic and buildings. (Try doing that in a rural area where yours may be the only car on the road that day.) When planning a surveillance operation or a raid in an urban environment, you may drive by the target area one or more times to recon the area or to look for someone in the area. You may not be able to do that on a secondary road in a rural area where everyone living on the road knows each other and a strange vehicle gets closely inspected.

I know of one county road that winds through one of the most beautiful areas in western North Carolina. It is the only road in and out of this area and several families live along it. You cannot drive through there without being noticed, and very likely all the folks along that road will know you are traveling through even before you pass their houses. Many of the people in this and other areas do not trust strangers and have a strong dislike for the government. This area is close to where the unsuccessful search for Eric Rudolph took place. This expensive and wasteful disaster was a prime example of how local rural residents, who may be helpful and supportive of local law enforcement, basically shut down when state and federal agencies rolled in.

THE HUNT FOR ERIC RUDOLPH

Eric Rudolph is suspected of planting bombs at the 1996 Olympics in Atlanta, Georgia, and at an abortion clinic in Alabama. Rudolph is a survivalist familiar with the mountains of western North Carolina. Retreating to these woods to hide, Rudolph eluded federal and state authorities and is still among the FBI's most wanted. At great expense to the American taxpayer, the FBI and

ATF conducted a search for Rudolph for more than a year before realizing they stood very little chance of finding him. To the members of the Southeast Bomb Task Force's credit, they did everything they possibly could to find this fugitive, but the bottom line is that they were conducting a massive operation that they were not trained to carry out. I visited the field headquarters they were working out of and discussed the search with several of the people in charge on a number of occasions. The FBI came away realizing that this was a classic example of trying to jam a square peg into a round hole.

I believe that the FBI did everything it thought was right in the search for the suspect. But I also am convinced the agents went about it the wrong way. The FBI, to my knowledge, does not train for and is not qualified to conduct rural operations. There is no question that it is one of the best law enforcement organizations in the world, but you cannot take a group of agents who may be the best in bank robbery investigations or fraud investigations, put them in camouflage fatigues, and expect them to operate well in mountainous terrain. They didn't know the area, they weren't trained for the mission, and it is a miracle someone wasn't permanently injured or killed during the search. I knew it was amateur night when I saw some of the searchers moving through the wooded areas. They weren't well camouflaged, they weren't looking around very well, their patrol security was next to nonexistent, and they did not know how to safely move through the terrain.

I knew they weren't going to be successful when I found out that they were not fully using the local sheriff's office to assist them in their operation. While the county sheriff had been assisting the FBI and the ATF by providing deputies to help with a number of administrative tasks and errands, such as accompanying agents interviewing local residents, for the most part it was a federal operation. The wide range of knowledge and expertise that existed in the sheriff's office went untapped. It wasn't my place to question their judgement but I knew personalities and egos were involved, and that is never a good thing for any operation, especially one as potentially dangerous as this one.

There was also a great deal of concern that Rudolph might have been hiding in a cave and that he may have booby-trapped some of the trails and the cave he was hiding in. I am not aware of whether any booby-trap training had been given to the teams searching in the area or not. I can only tell you that the few teams I saw moving in the area were not moving in such a way as to enable them to spot a booby trap, an ambush, or anything else. Many of these search teams were from large-city SWAT teams or were federal agents who spent most of their time working in cities and were detailed for a short period to aid in the search. They weren't familiar with the area and had not worked together in a rural environment. They were being tasked to do a job they weren't experienced in and, in many cases, weren't trained for.

But what really indicated to me that they would never find the suspect was what I was told on my last visit to the operations center. When I asked what time schedule their patrols were working on, I was told that they put them out around 8 or 9 in the morning and that they came back in around 4 or 5 in the afternoon. I then asked when the search teams went out at night. The agent in charge told me they didn't put anyone out at night. His words to me were, "Nobody can move out there once it gets dark." At first I thought he was making a joke, but when I realized that he was serious I knew there were serious problems and that the operation was fundamentally flawed. I tried to tell him that hunters, bear trappers, dope growers, and this suspect moved through the woods at night, but he didn't seem to want to accept that information. I knew then that I was possibly wearing out my welcome and they really didn't care to hear any of my ideas or advice. It was time for me to leave. To date, Eric Rudolph is still on the FBI's Ten Most Wanted Fugitives list.

He may have died or he may have escaped but he wasn't apprehended, and I have a good idea why. A large amount of money was wasted and good men spent a lot of time trying to do something they weren't trained to do. I remain convinced that if more reliance and trust had been placed with the local authorities the outcome might have been different.

MISTRUST OF GOVERNMENT

Culturally rural inhabitants have a distinct set of beliefs, values, and behaviors that characterize their attitude toward authorities. This will have a direct impact on police activities in the area. When planning a rural surveillance operation, it is imperative that you know as much as you possibly can regarding people's attitudes and what threats you might face. In rural areas, people depend more on themselves rather than on the government to handle all their problems. As a result they may be less trusting of government, particularly state and federal governments, which are seen as insensitive to local needs. The suspicions about a strong central government are as real today as at any time in our history. They reflect attitudes of rural residents, who are generally less supportive than urban residents of government programs that provide welfare.

In many rural areas, efforts to study crime and attitudes toward law enforcement have proven difficult because residents often try to keep community problems to themselves. This can lead people to depend on themselves to administer justice. It also leads to a greater mistrust of government representatives. Once, when operating in a rural area with some sheriff's deputies, I asked them if there was much crime in the area. The local deputy told me, "It's hard to say. We don't get too many calls out this way. If people have a problem, they tend to settle it themselves and we never hear about it from either side!" This attitude toward law enforcement can definitely pose a problem to officers who might be conducting rural surveillance in the same area.

Today there are many extremist groups operating in rural jurisdictions. Many of them are better armed than the local authorities.

CHANGES IN RURAL AMERICA

During the past decades, America's rural landscape has become dotted with extremists and survivalist training camps. A Ku Klux Klan-sponsored group in the Southwest has taught guerilla warfare tactics and techniques. A Christian survivalist school hidden deep in the Arkansas Ozark Mountains even taught urban warfare. Some rural areas have a long history of violence. Related to the issue of violence, though less documented, is the use of rural areas by "hate groups" and related extremist organizations. Aside from the physical isolation and privacy afforded by rural settings, rural culture has elements that are consistent with the mind-set of some right-wing extremist groups. But it is not exclusive to the right-wing elements. Some environmental extremist groups also use remote areas to train in.

Survivalists in particular see the urbanization of America as an evil thing. They set up communities in rural areas and espouse the return to a simpler life. There is nothing wrong with this until they commit crimes; then things become difficult for the local authorities. Some of these people resort to crime to sustain themselves and some have a belief that they are the only authority on the land that they occupy. Survivalists and other groups weave together violence and religion, believing that Armageddon is near. They preach that their survival requires them to be isolated and heavily armed. Many of them see themselves as highly patriotic and religious. Some of them use religious beliefs to justify racism and rationalize their defiance of the law.

These groups certainly have a right to exist and they have a right to live in rural areas. The problem comes when they commit crimes against others based on what they believe or to sustain their existence. What makes them so difficult to police is their isolation, distrust of the authorities, intimate knowledge of the area, and their strong (blind) belief that what they espouse is right. By all accounts these groups are increasing, not decreasing. As more groups

form, more problems for authorities and innocent citizens will arise.

TODAY'S PROBLEMS

As extremist groups move into and expand in rural areas, crime in these areas is likely to increase. It is obvious to me that most departments are not prepared to monitor what is taking place in large areas of their jurisdiction or to investigate potential criminal activities. Some of these problems have been longstanding, while we are just now becoming aware of others. If you think there aren't problems with crime in rural America or a dire need to be able to conduct rural surveillance's, read on.

- It has been documented that gang activity has taken place in rural areas, and there is a growing belief that some gangs may move more of their activities into rural areas.
- Drug activity is taking place throughout rural America. Whether it is drug use, production, shipment operations, or distribution, this will continue to grow.
- Crimes connected to tourism in rural areas have been a growing problem, and there is no reason to believe that this will not continue.
- Domestic violence is a growing crime in America, including rural areas.
- There has been a dramatic increase in crimes against the elderly and it is taking place in rural areas as well as in urban areas. Many older and retired Americans are moving to rural areas to escape crime in urban areas only to find some of the same problems in their new surroundings.
- Crime against minorities may often be more problematic in rural areas than in urban areas simply because there is less of a law enforcement presence.
- Training and manpower are a major problem for almost all local rural law enforcement authorities. As stated earlier, most departments lack the officers to cover the areas they are responsible for. They also

don't provide the training necessary to conduct a good rural surveillance operation.
- There is increasing growth of extremist and hate groups in rural areas.
- There is a lack of funding.

Given the fact that crime is only going to increase in rural American and the realization that most sheriff's offices are ill prepared to deal with these problems, it became necessary to develop a unique course of training and a book to augment this training. It is unlikely that we can get training to all of the departments that need it, but hopefully we can get them to read this book and inspire them to develop an in-house capability on their own. The best and most realistic solution to this problem, at least for the time being, is to be aware of the increasing crimes and threats, address the need for training, and increase the law enforcement presence in rural areas.

Note
1. *Dead drop* is a location or device used to leave or pick up messages or instructions from someone you do not want to risk having contact with, but need to communicate with. This term is often used in espionage.

Chapter Two:
Mission Planning
and Team Selection

- Is there a need for a rural surveillance operation?
- Has the decision been made to conduct the operation?
- Does the operation have the commitment from its leadership to fully support the operation?
- Have all the goals of the operation been clearly identified?

If you can answer yes to all these critical questions then it is time to get down to some serious planning. Keep in mind that the planning you do is in large part going to be based upon the objectives of the operation, so it is important that you get your objectives identified as clearly as possible from the start. They may change once planning begins, but you will find it very hard to conduct detailed planning if you aren't clear on what you are planning for.

As is often the case, you and your team may spend hours or even days or weeks planning to conduct a rural surveillance operation only to have the mission change at the last minute. I have seen situations where teams were en route to their drop-off points and had the objectives change. They ended up proceeding to the drop-off or insertion point and then making their adjustments once on the ground and in the operational area of the target. This is the sign of a dedicated, professional team that has trained and worked together in the past. That is why training and working together is critical to mission success.

WHAT DO WE HOPE TO GAIN?

Before beginning to plan for a rural surveillance operation it is imperative that we know what we hope to accomplish. Like the old man once said, "If you don't know where you want to go you'll probably never be able to get there." Likewise, you and the others planning and conducting rural surveillances will need to know what you hope to gain. Just as with any surveillance, there are a number of things a rural surveillance can accomplish for you. Here are some of the things you may be able to accomplish.

- Obtain evidence of a crime that has been committed
- Observe crimes actually being committed
- Check on the reliability/truthfulness of informants
- Obtain information on a location or individual
- Monitor the movements and activities of subversive persons
- Collect planning information for a raid or rescue operation
- Determine if a suspect is frequenting a certain location
- Observe a meeting or transaction between one or more suspects
- Curtail criminal activity
- Confirm an individual's whereabouts and activities
- Establish/verify a person's identity
- Identify a suspect's contacts or associates
- Obtain photographs for use as evidence

- Determine possible fraudulent insurance claims
- Prevent crimes before they actually take place
- Rescue a hostage

There are probably a half-dozen other reasons for conducting a discreet operation. Well organized and professionally conducted, a rural surveillance operation can reveal some extremely useful information that may make a major difference when a case goes to trial or you have to conduct a follow-up operation.

SELECTION OF PERSONNEL

Let's assume that all the questions at the beginning of the chapter were answered in the positive and that you have the full support of those in charge. You have a clear definition of what the mission is and what you want to accomplish and are now ready to begin your mission planning. Among the most critical elements of mission planning will be the selection of personnel. This includes not only the selection of the individuals who are going to be involved in the actual surveillance, but also the selection of those that are going to be in direct support of the team on the ground. For now let's discuss the selection of those individuals who are going to conduct the surveillance—the people who will be on the ground with their eyes on the target.

The main criterion is to select personnel who are highly motivated. Team members have got to want to be on the team. Their motivation has to be strong to the point that they are willing to work extra hours and make sacrifices, both professional and personal, to be part of a select professional group. This motivation also needs to be strong enough that they are willing to undergo physical hardships not normally required by other duties in their organization. Team members should always be volunteers. This is not the type of work someone should be volunteered for; that will possibly get other team members hurt and likely compromise the operation.

A rural surveillance team member should be mentally tough. This is hard to gauge if you don't know the volunteers well. And even if you think you know them, once people start experiencing the discomfort that a rural surveillance operation provides, they may react in ways that surprise you. I know people who are great officers and great investigators but when they have to spend more than a few hours in the woods, they start to act a little weird. You have to know the people you are going to send on an operation. That is why it is critical that the team members train together frequently under a variety of conditions. It is during this training that you will determine each other's mental toughness.

In addition to being highly motivated, team members must possess the ability to learn a variety of skills. They must also want to learn. I have seen a number of very smart people who possessed the intelligence to be great surveillance operators but didn't want to work at it. They only wanted the fun part and weren't willing to work and sacrifice to be really good. In addition to being a skilled law enforcement officer or investigator, members of a rural surveillance team need woodcraft skills that allow them to take care of themselves and their fellow teammates for extended times in the woods.

Team members must be able to rapidly compose themselves when becoming excited or facing fear or indecisiveness. Losing control of one's emotions, even for a few seconds, can be fatal or compromise an operation. All team members must have emotional balance and be able to calm their fears and imaginations.

Above all other qualities, when selecting a person for a rural surveillance team I would say trust, discipline, and maturity are the most important things to look for. If the candidate doesn't possess these, there really is no point in going any further. Operational security—the protection of information regarding the operation—is absolutely critical and will be discussed in detail later. However, if you have a team member who can't be trusted to keep quiet about an upcoming operation, then you might as well not have that person on the team.

Constant training builds a strong team and ensures mission success.

Candidates for your team should demonstrate the following characteristics:

- Have experience as a camper or hiker and enjoy being in the woods
- Have experience as a hunter or tracker
- Have a keen interest in photography
- Have an interest and good working knowledge of weapons
- Be able to make rapid, accurate assessments of a given situation
- Be emotionally stable
- Be able to function effectively under stress
- Have patience
- Be able to focus completely
- Be able to endure solitude and hours or days of boredom
- Be able to work under stress for an extended period
- Have strong physical conditioning
- Be free from the habits of smoking or drinking

- Be capable of working with another individual in a confined space
- Be able to evaluate a situation with objectivity
- Have a strong attention to detail
- Have a good memory
- Be able to accurately record in detail what they observe and hear

Finding dedicated personnel who will volunteer for rural surveillance operations and have the traits and characteristics above may not be easy, but it is better to have a good four- to six-man team with these qualities than to compromise your standards just for a larger team. Department personnel who have had experience as snipers or as members of SWAT teams sometimes make excellent rural surveillance operators, but not always. If they do not possess all of the attributes above they may compromise rather than strengthen a team.

Selecting team members is always a difficult job. No two rural surveillance operations are alike and may require a different team makeup each time. That is not to say that each operation won't have the entire team involved. It only means that the roles of who does what may be different depending on the circumstances and what strengths and weaknesses each team member has.

Some Key Ingredients

Judgement

It is absolutely necessary to select team personnel you know have sound judgement. They must be people who can evaluate a situation and make intelligent, unemotional decisions that will not compromise the operation or endanger the team. Due to the high risks of rural surveillance operations you can't afford someone with you who does stupid things. If it's a law enforcement operation you

may have to go to court, and you want people out there with you who aren't going to do something that might lose the case.

Patience

This one is critical. With any surveillance operation, patience is essential for everyone involved. Patience is also required in the people *supporting* a rural surveillance operation. I would say that patience is even more critical in a rural operation than an urban one because there is absolutely nothing to do while waiting for something to happen. Also, you may have to sit on a target for days before there is any activity at all.

Powers of Observation

This is a trait that has to be developed; it is not something that comes naturally to people and it is extremely important to those involved in a rural surveillance operation. If you can't observe every detail and activity of a target,

Training and rehearsals are essential.

16

there is no point in your being in the field. It is often the small things that most people miss that later prove to be critical. This is particularly true if you are collecting information that may be used to plan a raid or rescue operation later. People with good powers of observation work on developing the capability by continually closely observing people and things. You can train yourself to have this ability by observing things in detail. I often look at vehicles or people to see what distinguishing features they have that make them unique. Eventually you will find yourself doing this routinely and you will become a better observer of things around you.

Memory

When people make an effort to be aware and alert to objects and events around them, they begin to develop their ability to remember things. During a rural surveillance operation, you might not be able to use a radio or take notes without compromising yourself or the operation. It becomes critical that you are able to observe and remember everything that takes place. It is helpful to me to take a mental picture and then try to replay it over and over so it is clear in my mind until I have a chance to make notes about what I observed. (This can become difficult when you are tired.)

Attitude

I personally believe that if you don't have a team made up of individuals with strong, positive mental attitudes you may as well not even think about undertaking a rural surveillance operation. If operations are going to be difficult in any way—and almost all of them are—you will not succeed without a good attitude. When people get tired, hungry, and uncomfortable they begin to change. Your most eager team members may get the worst attitudes when things get difficult. Likewise, those whom you may have questioned and had concerns about will often surprise you and prove to be some of your most reliable members. People's real attitudes and character come out when they are tired and uncomfortable. This is why it is critical to work and train your rural surveillance team every chance you get. Learn whose attitude changes and what changes it. Knowing these things will pay off greatly when planning your operation.

Self-Confidence

Just as it is important that all rural surveillance team members have good attitudes, it is also important that they be self-confident. A person who is confident can think for himself and is much less likely to panic in a tight situation. However, it is important to remember that someone who is confident during a tense situation in an urban environment is not necessarily going to react the same way in a rural situation. In a place where there is no backup and the team is outnumbered, a completely different response may be generated. Again, this is where training will help you avoid a disaster on a real operation.

Physical Qualities

There are a number of physical attributes that may preclude someone from participating in an urban surveillance operation. Someone who is too big or too small, or has some unique physical quality that makes him conspicuous is not going to make a good operator. However, with rural surveillance, if you can avoid detection it doesn't matter if you are six-foot-eight or five-foot-two. As a matter of fact, being very small has distinct advantages in rural surveillance. What is critical is that you are in good physical condition, particularly with regard to endurance.

Good eyesight is extremely important. Team members should have regular eye checkups to test their ability to observe from a distance. It's OK to have a team member who requires glasses as long as his eyesight is correctable to 20/20. Just make sure he brings a second set of glasses on any operation. It is also important to have team members with good night vision. A diet deficient in vitamin A can lead to night blindness; make sure the people on your team eat well before and during the operation to ensure their night vision is adequate to carry out the operation. This is a team leader's responsibility.

Good hearing is also important to rural surveillance operations. There have been numerous operations where observers were close enough to those they were observing to hear most or all of the things being said. I can recall an operation where a team crawled beneath an outbuilding and could hear everything that was said in the area. Under good conditions you will be amazed at how far people's voices will carry. One of the good things about rural surveillance is that, due to remoteness of their location, the people being watched often speak and act freely because they don't think there is anyone else around. Make sure your people have their hearing checked. Anyone who doesn't get this done isn't serious about being on the team.

MISSION PLANNING

When beginning mission planning, these are the most important issues:

- What do you want to accomplish?
- What will it take?
- What is the risk versus the gain?

If possible, a survey of the target and/or the area should be created. This can be accomplished in a variety of ways but it may be dictated by the circumstances of the case you are working. If team members can conduct a drive-by or trips through the area, this pays big dividends and can eliminate a lot of unnecessary effort and planning. If you have access to an airplane or helicopter, that's even better. But don't do what I have seen people do too many times—they get in their car or in an aircraft and cruise into or over the area and don't start trying to figure where things are in relation to their maps until they're right over the target. For heaven's sake, do a map recon and get oriented before you even start thinking about going into the area. Once, in the late 1970s, an intelligence team was conducting an aerial surveillance

along the East German border. As its members were trying to get oriented, their maps—with sensitive markings on them—went out the aircraft window. They were flying under 2,000 feet altitude and—you guessed it—the maps went floating into East Germany!

When conducting a preliminary survey be prepared and know what you should be looking for. What types of clothing do people wear and what stands out? What types of vehicles fit in and what stands out? What is different from the information your maps show? Where are the possible vantage points? You may have a team member or trusted source who is familiar with the area, but try to verify their information whenever possible. Your situation may be such that you can't conduct a recon before beginning the operation. If this is the case, at least do a good map recon and be sure that every member of the team is also familiar with the maps of the area you will be using.

Prior to beginning any rural surveillance operation, and throughout the entire planning process, there are a number of points that should be continually reviewed:

- Is all intelligence/information on the target?
- What are the ultimate mission objective(s)?
- What do you want to accomplish?
- Are you capable of achieving it?
- What are the risk factors to the public and the team?
- What's the strategy—have you overlooked anything?
- What are your needs and resources?
- How is security—has the plan been compromised?

As you begin your mission planning, it is important that you designate one key person to consolidate all your operational information on the area and target. Too often several people, all with the best of intentions, end up compiling the same information. Each person thinks the other is disseminating the information and it never gets put into the planning process. Have one focal point that all intelligence and information goes to. This should be the one person that all people, including the team leader, go to for updates. One way to decide if information is important is to keep asking the following questions:

- Who are we working against?
- What do we expect them to do?
- When is it likely to happen?
- Where are they likely to do it?
- Why is it likely to happen?
- How do we think they will do it?

The function of your surveillance operation may be to fill in some of the answers to these questions.

The Decision Making Process

You might want to use the following guidelines to govern your decision making process. These answers will be useful throughout your mission-planning sequence. Remember, just as the mission-planning process is continuing and evolving, so too is the decision making process. As you plan you are still reviewing the decision to conduct the mission as new information becomes available.

- Identify the problem. This can quickly change.
- Decide on the objectives of the rural surveillance. This list may change as well.
- Analyze risk. This is ongoing during the operation.
- Decide on acceptable risks and losses.
- What could cancel the operation?
- Get any questions regarding legal issues answered before you begin.

Mission Preparation and Planning

Operational Timing

There are many factors that can influence timing; each situation is different. You may have a hostage rescue situation that calls for immediate action, with no time to conduct surveillance of a target. There will also be times when you have plenty of options of when to

conduct the surveillance and you can pick and choose when to begin. In addition to the situation, which will always dictate your operational timing, there a numerous other factors that might determine when you conduct the operation, including:

- Weather
- Moon phase
- Availability of personnel
- Legal issues/rulings
- Target's activities
- Foliage

Use of Available Time

This is a mission-planning consideration that I have seen overlooked too many times. Time and again good teams fail to use the time available to fully plan and prepare for an operation. Even the best teams get overconfident and feel that they can wait until the last minute to plan for an operation, as when they are going back to a target they have surveilled before and feel they don't really need to plan for the same thing again. Nothing could be further from the truth. Every rural surveillance operation is different. Even if you are returning to a target you have been on several times before there is going to be something different. I can recall a target I had gone to more than five times; each time there were several things that were different and each of those things could have compromised the mission if we hadn't been prepared for them. Never forget Murphy's Law—if something can go wrong, it will. Use all the time you have available to plan and prepare for your surveillance operation. There is always something else you can do to be better prepared.

Staff Roles and Limits

You need to decide exactly who is responsible for what, and each person needs to get his share of the good and the bad. Make sure that as each team member is given duties and responsibility for mission planning and preparation, you don't keep sticking the same people with the same jobs. It's true that you want to have tasks assigned to the person best suited for the job, but at the same time remember even the best team members can become complacent if they do the same thing over and over. Have team members cross-trained so there is always a backup and no one gets tired of doing the same job all the time.

Administrative Support

The person or persons assigned to provide administrative support are going to be critical for a number of reasons. First, if at all possible, the administrative support people need to be members of the team. If this is not possible, they need to be people you can completely trust. They are going to have a lot of information about what your team is doing and if they can't be trusted to keep it confidential and protected, then you are finished before you begin. Also, even the best plan in the world can fail if the administrative requirements are not taken care of. The people providing this support need to be trustworthy, security-conscious, reliable, and sticklers for detail. Keep in mind that even after the mission is completed, there is still an administrative job to do.

Briefing Mission and Support Personnel

As you begin your mission planning and preparation you must thoroughly brief your personnel. You may want to brief the mission or team personnel separately from your support personnel, depending on the particular situation. What information you discuss during these briefings is up to you and your supervisor, but remember that you will need to give team members enough detailed information for them to do their jobs and to prepare for the upcoming operation.

I can remember a surveillance operation that was highly classified. The brass decided to alert team members, but all the higher ups would tell them was that they had a possible operation coming up in the next several weeks and to be prepared to leave on short notice. The brass were so concerned about security that they wouldn't discuss any of the details, yet

they expected the team to start detailed planning. Of course that couldn't happen, and as a result valuable time was lost. It is fine to be security conscious but not to the point that you restrict the very people who have to conduct the operation.

Map and Area Study

This is critical when planning and preparing for a rural surveillance operation. Obviously one of the first things you have to do is make sure that you have the most current maps of your operational area available. Too many times I have seen teams conduct mission planning using maps that were old and inaccurate. I have also seen maps that hadn't been updated in more than 10 years but were accurate as the day they were printed, but you can't count on that. Get the most current map information for your team. Professional rural surveillance teams in a sheriff's office will periodically update their maps to ensure that they have the most current information. Also, it is important to have area study information available for the team. This is critical for the team and will be discussed in detail in future sections.

Coordinating Support

Even the best teams need support from other sources from time to time, especially if they are going to be conducting a rural surveillance for more than just a few days. They may even need to coordinate support if the operation is only going to last a few hours. Your team may need to have an emergency vehicle in position for a critical point in the operation, or have a helicopter on call in the event of a crisis. This may be arranged with another law enforcement department or with assets in a neighboring municipality.

As with any other part of planning and preparation, security must have the highest priority but don't be so paranoid that you don't get the support you need to ensure your success. Your administrative support person may handle much of the mission's coordination—this is why the reliability of that

Select team members who are 100 percent dedicated.

person is so important. If it is possible to prearrange some of your mission support or to have a type of mutual aid agreement established before an operation comes up, all the better.

Personnel Selection

Available Assets

You have to plan and work with who and what is available; this is one reason it is so important to cross-train your personnel. If your best point man or map reader is on vacation or sick with the flu when your biggest rural surveillance operation comes up, you'll need to have another team member take his place.

The people you select should be tailored to fit the requirements of the operation. One mistake I have seen made time and again is planners' letting personalities and

relationships determine who will go on an operation rather than selecting the best person for a particular operation.

Experience and Training

When selecting personnel for a rural surveillance operation, make absolutely certain that they have been trained and have demonstrated that they can actually do the job. There are a lot of people that say they can navigate in the woods or that they are good trackers, but when they get on the ground you quickly find out they only thought they could do it.

Medical Considerations

This one is critical. Whether you are the leader of a rural surveillance team, the team medic, or just one of the team members, it is imperative that you know the medical conditions of your fellow team members. Why is this important? Well, you wouldn't want someone with a bad knee serving on point in rugged mountainous conditions or someone with limited visual capabilities manning an observation point a long distance from the target. Someone with serious allergies could be compromised during hay fever season.

The point here is that the team leader must know the strengths and limitations of his team members. Someone's medical condition can change fast, so stay current on team members' medical status. This is also something that should be reviewed during early mission planning; don't wait until you are loading up and getting ready to find out if someone has a problem.

Psychological Considerations

Don't neglect this one. There are a lot of good people who want to be on a rural surveillance team; however, there are few who are really going to be able to cope with the unusual demands a long-term operation requires.

Whenever I think about this I am reminded of the deputy who freaked out when he walked into a snake hanging in some vines one night. (We're still not sure that it really was a snake, but he thought it was.) It got to him so badly that he quit and left that night. Fortunately it was just a training exercise, and the incident showed us that he really didn't belong on the team. This was our third day of training, and this individual seemed to be the hardest charging guy out there. You just never know.

Some people can't function without a crutch. I once had to medevac a senior NCO who "lost it" because he ran out of cigarettes. We found him at sundown after looking for him most of the day. He was sitting at the base of a large tree staring off and mumbling to himself. He could not handle being alone and without his smokes for an extended period. He was a good man and during Vietnam served in Special Forces in Laos and North Vietnam, but he had gotten to where he just couldn't deal with being alone in the woods for a long time. You must get to know your people and how they will perform under the conditions of a rural surveillance operation.

Weapons and Equipment Selection

Issued Weapons

It may be your decision or department policy that determines what weapons will be taken on a rural surveillance. I would say that the weapon selection should be made based on the worst possible threat. The advantage to taking issued weapons—those for everyday use—is that they are the ones the team members are most likely familiar and proficient with.

Special Weapons

The mission and the possible threats that may exist in the area under surveillance should determine the need for special weapons. Just make sure that the weapons selected pass the common-sense test: *There is absolutely no sense in taking weapons you will not need to accomplish your mission or protect yourself.* Also, keep in mind that the more different weapons you take, the more different types of ammunition you have to carry.

I went out with one team that brought along a scoped sniper rifle. (While I knew we would not be doing any sniper ops, I do think having a sniper covering a surveillance team is a good practice.) When I asked why they were bringing the weapon, they said because they wanted to use the detachable rifle scope. I decided to let them learn the lesson the hard way, and they did within 24 hours of moving the unwieldy gun through dense brush.

If the situation on a target allows it and you have the manpower, having a security or overwatch team with special weapons, such as a sniper weapon, may be a good idea. Any time you can increase the security for the team surveying the target, do so. Just be certain that any special weapons you take along, whether they are shotguns, machine guns, or stun grenades, will serve a real purpose.

Team Equipment

The equipment you issue to all team members should also pass the common-sense test. Make sure that every bit of equipment you issue has a purpose; don't issue useless gadgets just because the department got them for a bargain. Establish your team equipment list based on what works best in your area and what is really useful. I have listed here some items for you to consider—it is by no means complete, and you will need to expand on it based on your particular situation.

- Compass
- Individual first-aid kit
- Two 2-quart canteens
- Good field knife, such as a KA-BAR
- Binoculars
- Leather gloves
- Camouflage stick/paint
- Poncho and liner
- Space blanket
- Ground pad
- Backpack with padded shoulder straps
- Emergency rations and signal mirror
- Twelve feet of parachute suspension cord

You should constantly review and improve this list for your team. *Always* conduct an inspection prior to deploying to ensure that all team members have the items they are supposed to have.

Individual Equipment

This is an area that is left to the discretion of the individual team member, but the team leader must also have some input. What you may want to restrict is anything that is brightly colored and will not blend into the environment. Also, anything that might break or rattle could compromise the team or team member. A team leader needs to make sure his people are not taking foods that are high in salt content; that they have enough water; that they don't bring items with strong scents; and that they aren't bringing things that will spoil or attract animals. Here is a sample of things to consider.

- Bug repellant
- Towel in an earth tone
- Pocket knife
- Several pairs of padded socks
- Multi-vitamins
- Sharpened pencils and a note pad

After several training exercises, team members will quickly learn what things to bring to the field and what they don't need and don't want to carry!

Camping Gear

Although extended rural surveillance operations may be camping trips of a sort, they aren't like the trips most people know. Your team may have to set up a base camp constructed to blend in with the surroundings. It can't be easily approached, and must be made to be packed up and moved quickly. Rather than having tents, small lean-tos may have to be built. Colorful backpacks can't be used—anything that shines or reflects light or makes noise must be excluded. Camping stoves and fires have to be banned; the smoke or smell may alert others in the area. Some of the best gear for these types of operations may be found in military surplus stores or camping and hunting stores. It may take trial and error to find what works best for you.

Survival Gear

A personal survival kit can come in many sizes with varying contents. It does not need to be elaborate but it does need to be functional. When designing your survival kit, keep in mind that it is only to be used in the event of an emergency or survival situation. The container you decide to use should be camouflaged, waterproof, durable, and easy to carry. What you choose to include in your survival kit is an individual choice but the contents should fall into six categories:

- First-aid items, including antibiotic ointment
- Signaling items
- Water purification
- Fire-starting items
- Food
- Shelter items

Remember that anyone can become disoriented and lost in the woods, so don't ignore the requirement for a survival kit. Also keep the kit with you at all times while on an operation.

Medical Equipment

The nature of the mission, type of area you will operate in, and the special needs of your team determines the type of team medical equipment you take with you. If you are fortunate enough to have an EMT (emergency medical technician) or other medically trained personnel on your team, take advantage of their knowledge.

While in the army I was fortunate to have Special Forces medics who knew their stuff and took care of all team medical requirements. One thing they always made sure of was that team members carried their individual medical kits with them and that they had any prescription needs with them in waterproof containers. The medics also carried backups for each team member just in case. As a minimum, make sure all members of the rural surveillance team have individual first-aid kits and that they receive basic first-aid training. In the field first-aid chapter, you will find a list of suggested kit contents.

Recording Methods

With today's technology there is no shortage of great camera and video gear available for rural surveillance operations, but there are important things to remember about today's technology. First of all, it is *very* sensitive to moisture. If you are going to be out overnight, you will encounter some type of moisture. Also, dust and dirt can cause this equipment to malfunction. Any operation that lasts more than several hours requires backup batteries. I believe if you find some good low-light camera gear that does the job, you should by all means use it. Some of the new Sony 8mm 1-lux or no-lux cameras are great and you can waterproof them. Make certain to cover all reflective surfaces on the gear; this has given away the position of more than one team.

I also recommend having team members sketch the target in detail when they are observing a target for any period. Then if the film is lost there will still be a record. Sketching also helps to keep the team focused on the target. These sketches should *always* be drawn in pencil and never in pen. Pencil will last longer, can be erased for a correction and won't run if it gets wet like ink will. (Be smart enough to bring several sharpened pencils.)

Communications

I have mixed feelings about communications equipment; with technology today this is a double-edged sword. You need to have good communications gear with the team but the bad guys today may have the scanning equipment to pick up your transmissions. I recommend that you have your own internal team communication methods that can be used to call in support and backup if you need it.

However, being from the old school, I recommend you not use radio communications except in an emergency. If you have planned your operation well and carry it off successfully there are ways to operate successfully without

sending any radio messages. This is something I always emphasize when teaching this course. You can do this and still let your support team know you are OK and when to pick you up. This takes training and practice, but it can be done and should become part of your team operating procedures.

There are a number of ways a team can communicate that everything is going as planned. For example, if it is operating near a road, it can leave a prearranged signal by the road at certain intervals, such as a specific piece of litter or survey tape. A simple predetermined squelch on a radio can also be used as a type of signal, and answered back the same way. There are any number of methods, limited only by the imagination of the team.

Vehicle Support

The vehicles used to support your operation need to be rugged and have enough cargo room for transporting team members and gear as well as allow quick entry and exit. What's most important is that vehicles fit in and don't attract attention. You shouldn't try to deliver a rural surveillance team to an area using a squad car or open pickup truck; having the wrong type of vehicle can quickly compromise a mission and get team members hurt. Also, the vehicles need to be committed to the operation for its entire duration and only the mission support should have access to the vehicle during this time.

If your team has the luxury of being able to modify a vehicle for this purpose, all the better. Large vehicles that can carry a team of five to eight men with equipment are ideal. Chevy Suburbans or Ford Expeditions are good for this type of operation. The vehicle needs to be padded and taped to keep the noise down, and there will need to be light controls for the brakes and interior lights. The vehicle entry/exit procedures must be rehearsed several times to allow team members to get it down to the point that it only takes a few seconds for them to enter or exit the vehicle quietly without detection.

Aerial Support

If you have the opportunity for aerial support there are several ways you can use it. First, it is a great asset to use to check the accuracy of your maps. Second, if you have plenty of advance warning before an operation, you can fly over or near the target days or weeks before you go in. This aerial recon could do a lot to aid you in your operational planning. An aerial recon at night can let you know if a target is occupied at night.

It would not be a good idea to conduct too many over flights if the mission is sensitive, as the target might become suspicious. Also, if the target is in an area where aircraft rarely or never fly, then the risk probably outweighs the gain. This is one of those options that depends on the situation.

Detailed Planning

Intelligence Estimates

For the purpose of conducting rural surveillance this comes in the form of area study and reconnaissance. It means studying the area by any and all means at your disposal. This may be done by one or more vehicle recons through the area. Although this may be beneficial, it may also be very risky depending on the type of target you're working against and the area you're operating in. A vehicle reconnaissance may also give a false sense of what you will encounter. I recall a time when we were going to take a team in and we drove through the area for a quick look. The road paralleled the route we were going to take and from the road it looked fairly easy. A look at the map indicated it was much worse than it appeared from the road—and it was! Never depend solely on a drive-by recon if you can help it.

Maps can be great sources of information about what might be encountered in the area. Even old maps are useful; terrain usually remains the same for decades. If you can conduct an aerial recon to check against your map information, all the better. But be sure to study your maps *before* you conduct any aerial reconnaissance.

Your area study should include the following:

- Availability and quality of water in the area
- Food sources
- Natural threat areas (swamps, flood plains, cliffs, and gorges)
- Natural threats (wildlife, weather)
- Current or recent land use
- Attitudes/beliefs of those living in the area
- Economic situation of the region
- Cover and concealment

Information on the area might also be obtained through members of your organization or people that you trust who live in or near the area or are familiar with it. But you must use extreme caution when going outside your team to gather information about the target area: Unless you can be absolutely certain of the reliability of an individual, don't use him as a source of information. Remember that once you commit a rural surveillance team to a target area, it is extremely vulnerable. You may not be able to assist it right away and if it is compromised, there could be a disaster.

Operations Estimate and Plan

Here is where you should make your estimate of the threat and likelihood of success as well as your detailed operational planning. Based upon the objectives of the operation and information from your intelligence estimate, you can make an honest appraisal of your chances of success. Much of the planning here will be dictated by your team's standing operating procedures (SOP). Any modifications to that will be as the result of a unique situation. It is here that you should plan for any unforeseen situations where you have to modify or cancel the operation altogether.

Logistics Requirements

Your logistics requirements are critical to the success of your surveillance operation, and it cannot be overemphasized how much thought you must put into planning.

The type of surveillance, the threat you may be facing, and the duration of the operation are all factors as you determine your logistics requirements. The best way to ensure that you have anticipated all your needs is for the entire team to talk through each and every activity you will be engaged in or can imagine taking place from the moment you deploy on the operation until you have returned. As you discuss each step of the operation, list all the items each individual and the team as a whole will need to carry out the operation. If there are items you may need to have "on call" to be delivered to you during the operation, list those as well. It is important to think of all the things that could go wrong during the operation and what you would need in the event that the worst-case scenario took place. I strongly recommend that you "worst-case" things as you conduct your planning and coordination for logistics requirements. Remember, it is always better to have something and not need it than to need something in an emergency and not have planned for it.

Reporting Procedures

Although this part of the operation may not require a lot of detailed planning, it is critical during the operation as well as when the operation is completed. If this isn't done right the whole mission may be for nothing. Make sure it is clear to all team members what their reporting responsibilities are and to whom they are to pass on any information. I have seen short-term surveillance in which valuable information was lost because the team members were not briefed on what was expected of them. Although reporting procedures may be outlined in your SOP, review them each time. The first time you don't will be the time that the operation dictates you modify your procedures. These procedures should not only cover how, when, and what you will report during the surveillance, they should also cover procedures back to higher authorities. Long-term surveillance that doesn't get information back to those who need it is a wasted effort.

Infiltration Plan

Without a well-thought-out and well-rehearsed infiltration plan your operation may be compromised before it really begins. Different factors will determine how you will infiltrate the target area. Although it may take a little more time and effort, and sometimes be a bit risky, I believe that the more unlikely and difficult routes to a target are usually the best. Weather and moon phases may play an important part in the planning if you have the luxury of choosing your time to infiltrate.

It is vital that you select the right type of vehicles to get the team to the insertion or drop-off point. The vehicle or vehicles need to blend into the area as much as possible. This is a critical portion of any operation—and if not carried out the right way can lead to compromising the operation and the team before it even begins.

Procedures in the Target Area

Once the team has been successfully inserted into the target area it must move with caution and stealth. This is where training and teamwork pays off. The mission, terrain, weather, size of the team, and some other factors will dictate what actions the team takes. Here are some of the procedures a team should plan and train for:

- Order of movement and formations while moving
- Security while stopped or resting
- Hand and arm signals
- Actions if the team is compromised
- Actions if the team is attacked
- Alternative plans
- Base camp procedures (setup, security, housekeeping)
- Noise and light discipline
- Emergency evacuation
- Resupply procedures
- Sanitizing the area
- Withdrawal from the area

There are likely many more that may need to be established for a team based on individual circumstances, but these and any others need to be clearly established, practiced, and understood by everyone on the team.

Departing the Target Area

In many ways, departure may be more important to train for than insertion simply because once it's time to leave and get out of there, one of the first things that happens is that people start forgetting about security.

I was with a team once that arrived at its pickup point several hours early and was sitting too close to a road in minimal vegetation that gave very little cover. By arriving early, it was near the road at a time when there was a lot of traffic due to people traveling to work. Had the team stuck to its original plan, which took into account the traffic pattern in the area, it would not have been at such a high risk of being spotted.

As the sun rose, the team members became more and more exposed. Due to sparse cover they were in great danger of being detected as they moved out of the pickup area and back into denser cover. Fortunately, they were not detected. If they had been, the pickup site would have been compromised and the entire operation and the team would have been put at great risk.

Although the team members were not compromised, they had forgotten a very important point: the operation is not successfully completed until the entire team is out of the operational area. Exactly what that area is needs to be determined at the beginning of planning the operation. It would have been a shame for all the work and effort put into the operation to be lost because the team let its guard down at the last minute.

When departing the area, it is critical that all team members ensure they leave no obvious signs that they have been there. You can't be in an area for any period without leaving some signs, but there are a lot of things you can do to make sure those signs are kept to a minimum. Every team member needs to ensure there is no trash, equipment, or man-made material left in the area. Food or food wrappers, pencils or writing material, cords or strings, or anything else that is not natural and from the area can compromise an operation, even if the operation is over. If you are collecting data to plan a raid and leave signs you were there it could compromise the raid.

Extraction Plan

Just like the infiltration, your team's extraction must be planned in detail and rehearsed until it becomes second nature. If at all possible, plan your extraction site in a remote area where it would be difficult for anyone to observe you leaving. This isn't always possible, but in most rural areas there are locations that provide some cover for this part of the operation.

Keep in mind that your team is going to be extremely vulnerable at this point in the operation. The members will be tired and probably in an area they are not familiar with. Again, it is important that you have a vehicle with the capacity to carry the entire team, rigged to aid in noise and light discipline, and that can blend into the area. Your drivers for both the infiltration and extraction are a crucial part of your support planning. If your team and vehicle(s) are large enough so that security can accompany the driver, all the better. But do not risk a second pickup to have this luxury unless the situation absolutely dictates it.

You will need a way of signaling the driver that the team is in the area and ready to be picked up. If the pickup is going to take place at night or during limited visibility, you also need to plan for the driver to be able to signal the team that all is clear and that he is in fact the pickup vehicle. Always remember in your planning that what can go wrong will go wrong at the worst possible time. In rural surveillance operations, one of the worst possible times is during the extraction.

I once saw a vehicle approach a pickup site and the team member start to come out on the road only to find that it was not their pickup but a vehicle very similar to it. Fortunately for this team, the driver did not see them and they quickly recognized it wasn't their ride out of the area. The right vehicle came by a few minutes later and the team wasn't compromised. The team members had not planned for this event and it almost cost them. Make sure the driver is reliable and understands the importance of this portion of the operation.

Rehearsals

Equipment Checks

It is the responsibility of every team member to ensure that all his equipment is checked before each and every operation, even if it is just a training exercise!

If a team member is going to be using or carrying equipment that the entire team will be using such as spotter scopes, binoculars, or cameras, it is his responsibility to check that equipment. Never assume that it is functioning correctly or that someone else has checked it. Also, it is the team leader's responsibility to ensure that these checks are made.

As humans, we are basically lazy and we often rationalize that if our equipment was OK the last time it must be OK this time. I have lost count of how many times I have seen or heard about someone who went out and later realized he didn't have what he thought he had or something was broken or worn out. Each and every time *check all your equipment before you begin!*

Weapon Checks

This one is obviously critical but you would be amazed at how many people fail to test-fire their weapons before going on a rural surveillance operation. Granted, if you do things right you won't need your weapon, but when you need it you *really* need it. Test-fire and check all your weapons before leaving.

Communications Checks

Whether it is internal team communications or communications back to a support element or headquarters, this check is vital. If things go really wrong you must have a way of getting backup support as soon as possible. If the operation is expected to last for several days or

weeks you will need good communications for support and resupply. Also, your supervisor must have a way of knowing that everything is going according to plan and that the team is all right. I am not a big fan of having a lot of talk on the radio, and with the technology that the bad guys have today talking on the radios can compromise you. But you do need a system to communicate when you need to. There are ways to do this without giving your operation away. In any event be certain you know all your communications are working. Have spare radios, if possible, and plenty of batteries.

Security Checks and Actions

Every good rural surveillance team has trained and rehearsed in the field many times. If it knows what it doing, it has frequently rehearsed the security and immediate action drills it will employ while on an operation. The security checks and actions a team takes will depend on a number of variables such as the mission, size of the team, and terrain. Each team has its own tactics and procedures it prefers. It is enough to say here that these need to be reviewed and rehearsed prior to each operation. They should include how security will be covered as well as what actions to take if ambushed, compromised, etc.

Vehicle Exits and Entries

When a team enters and exits an area where the rural surveillance operation will take place it usually travels at least partway to the site in a vehicle. As discussed earlier, this should be a vehicle that blends into the area and is modified to facilitate the insertion and recovery of the team or teams. The rehearsal of this process is critical and needs to be done repeatedly. It is amazing how many things you didn't count on that you will find during these rehearsals that can screw up the insertion or extraction.

Remember that there is almost always something not thought of or overlooked, and the only way for it to show is by doing lots of rehearsals under conditions like those you will encounter on the operation.

In one particular case, we rehearsed 10 or 12 times and thought everything was rigged correctly—only to find out on the last try that we had not anticipated a key element: if we loaded the vehicle in the order we had been using, we lacked real security to provide cover as the vehicle was being loaded. As a result of rehearsing each step and thinking about what was the worst thing that could happen, we realized how vulnerable the team would be as it was trying to leave the area. By making a minor adjustment in the order that we loaded the team, we were able to eliminate this vulnerability. As your team actually walks through the steps it plans to take on an operation, corrections to potential problems can be discovered and eliminated.

If the team is going to be inserted at night, practice it over and over at night. Also, don't make the mistake of rehearsing the insertion and not rehearsing the extraction. Teams have made the mistake of thinking they will just reverse the process and it will work out, only to find out that there was something they had not accounted for. *Always rehearse!*

Briefing the Operation

This is one area often overlooked or not given much emphasis by a team. I recall one team that was ready to go on a challenging surveillance operation on the home of a drug dealer that the team had been after for some time. It was a good team and it had prepared for the operation. But the afternoon before it was to leave, it briefed the two senior people in the department. The briefing the team gave was not organized or well thought out and it gave the *appearance* that the team was not organized, so the senior officials called off the operation. I don't blame the sheriff that called it off; from his viewpoint, the team was not ready to go against a very dangerous target and he wanted to be sure it had its stuff together. The team didn't need to give a big dog and pony show, but should have given an organized briefing.

Attendees

It is critical that *only* those people who need to be there are there. The briefing of a rural surveillance operation is not the time to have every curious person in a 5-mile radius sitting in and listening to your plans. Make sure you have the support of the senior management on this issue prior to setting up the briefing. It's a good idea to hold this briefing in the chief's or sheriff's office or at a secure offsite location.

Security Warning

Don't be shy about giving a security warning to everyone in the briefing. If someone shows up late and you have to allow him in, make sure he is given a security warning as well. Do not hesitate to do this, no matter what his position is. Remember, you are presenting information that if compromised could cause you and your team to be injured or worse.

Mission Statement and Goals

It is important to state the mission and the goals of the operation at the beginning and again at the end of the operational briefing. This eliminates any uncertainty regarding what you and your team are trying to accomplish. It also helps to emphasize why it is necessary to conduct a rural surveillance operation.

Team Members

It is a good idea to have team members involved in giving portions of the operational briefing. It ensures that they understand the details of the operation and gives them the experience of conducting this type of briefings in the event the team leader is unable to make the presentation.

Rules of Engagement

This one can be tricky and will, of course, be dictated by the situation and the laws governing the jurisdiction where the operation will take place. It is important to include these factors in the briefing if only to ensure that all team members understand what action to take or not. It also serves to inform the brass about what actions you may need to take and lets them know you have planned for contingencies.

Support Requirements

During the briefing it is important to make clear what support you and your team need to accomplish the mission. This is not a time to be shy or to try to do everything on your own. If the briefing is for the purpose of getting a decision to conduct the operation, be very clear and concise on what you need to do the job. Make it clear what it will take in terms of equipment, personnel, and command support.

Estimated Risks and Success

Part of the briefing should include an honest assessment of all the risks involved and the estimated chance of success. Often a team will try to minimize the risks or inflate the potential for success in order to get approval to conduct an operation. This isn't fair to the leadership and it isn't fair to the team members who are putting themselves at risk. Give a fair and accurate assessment. If you have a well-trained team and you have planned the operation well, your chances of success are likely to be very high anyway, but always give an honest estimate.

Operational Security

Need-to-Know Rule

Rigidly enforce this rule! Unless someone has an absolute reason to know about an operation, don't tell him. If you have people on the team who can't keep their mouths shut and talk about operations, get rid of them immediately. If someone who does not have a need to know disseminates operational information, investigate aggressively and fix the leak.

Personal Emergencies

All good team members and leaders know their team mates well. They know their likes, dislikes, and much about their personal lives. It is very important that in your operational planning you develop contingencies for personal emergencies. If a team member has a family emergency, you need to have plans for getting him out of the operation without shutting the operation down.

Mission Debriefing

Even the best teams often don't adequately plan or practice for the critical and valuable portion of a mission that deals with team and individual debriefings. Countless times in my military, law enforcement, and even business experience I have seen lip service paid to thorough debriefings only to see valuable information lost due to neglect or other priorities. Part of your operational planning must be mission debriefings, both real as well as training. Remember that it has been proven time and time again that you execute as you train. If you don't conduct debriefings in training you probably won't do them following a real mission.

Responsibilities

It should be clearly defined who is responsible for conducting the debriefings and what type of report is expected. If there is a problem of cooperation, then that should very quickly become a leadership issue. When people return from a difficult operation the last thing they want to do is deal with a debriefing. They want to get home, clean up, and probably get some sleep or other comforts of home. If no one is responsible for making a debriefing happen it probably won't, so assign this responsibility at the beginning of operational planning.

Surveillance Reports

It is necessary to determine in your plan what format you want to use for reports and how often you want to consolidate these on an operation. I have seen it done a number of ways, and the way that seems to work best is to collect the report from each team as it comes back to the base camp and to consolidate them on a 24-hour basis.

If you have more than one hide site or team observing the target, it is a good idea to compare the reports to see if they are reporting the same activities at the same times. If the teams are reporting the same activity there is no point in reporting it twice in the mission debriefing, but it is critical to note that the information was confirmed by more than one team. This can be important if the surveillance reports lead to an arrest and a trial. Accuracy is critical, and the time to consolidate the information is right after the team comes off its surveillance watch.

Questionnaires

These may prove useful for a team to make sure it doesn't miss covering any areas and to establish a procedure for conducting its mission debriefings.

Lessons Learned

Questionnaires can also assist the team in conducting a lessons-learned session. This should be an ongoing process and is the sign of a committed and dedicated team. I have never been involved in a surveillance operation or a training session where I didn't learn at least one thing I didn't know before or wasn't reminded of something important I had forgotten. These lessons learned must be shared with all team members in a setting where questions and comments can be made. It should serve as a learning opportunity for all team members.

Follow-Up Actions

There must be follow-ups to correct team performance if necessary. This is everyone's responsibility, but the team leader may have to give the job of fixing the problem to one or more individuals. What is important is to take any corrective action before the next operation comes up.

Briefing Command Personnel

In addition to debriefing all the team and support personnel, it's important to provide this information to the organizers. Let them know what went right, what went wrong, and what help you need to make things better the next time. If your surveillance operations are collecting good information and helping to make cases, you should be able to get the support you need to do a better job in the future. The results of your mission debriefings need to be shared with those who can benefit from them and who can help you as a result of the information they provide. Make sure that in your mission planning you include you mission debriefings as part of the overall operation.

Chapter Three: Field First Aid

If you spend any amount of time in the woods, sooner or later you are going to have some type of injury. When you are involved in training or conducting a rural surveillance operation in which you are out for an extended period of time, carrying weapons and equipment and crawling around and hiding in the brush, your odds of an injury are going to be dramatically increased. This chapter deals with some of the more likely injuries you might encounter and what you can do to prevent and treat them.

The information here was taken from first-aid manuals, including the American Heart Association manual for first aid. This chapter is by no means comprehensive, but will hopefully serve as valuable information for you and your team. I strongly encourage any rural surveillance team to have as many team members as possible become EMT-qualified. All rural surveillance teams should include field first aid and emergency first-aid training in their schedule.

ANIMALS

Insect Bites and Stings

Most insect bites or stings are not life threatening; however, some can cause severe pain and illness, or even death if an allergy is present. If there is no allergic reaction first aid is a simple process, but the bite should be examined as soon as possible by medical personnel.

With less serious bites, there is pain, irritation, swelling, heat, redness, and/or itching. Hives may occur in the area of the bite accompanied by itching. These are the least severe of the allergic reactions and are usually not dangerous unless they affect the air passages. Bites and stings from bees, wasps, ants, mosquitoes, fleas, and ticks are usually not serious and the irritation normally stays localized in the area of the bite. If a team member has an allergic reaction, he should receive medical care immediately.

Spider bites can also be very serious. A bite from the black widow can affect the nervous system, causing cramps, a rigid non-tender abdomen, breathing difficulties, sweating, nausea, and vomiting. Venom from the brown recluse spider usually produces local rather than system-wide problems; however, tissue damage around the area of the bite can be severe and if left untreated can cause an ulcer, loss of tissue, and even gangrene.

First Aid
There are certain basic principles that apply regardless of what caused the bite or sting:

- If there is a stinger present, remove it by scraping the surface of the skin with a fingernail, knife, or firm piece of plastic (such as a credit card). Scrape away from the bite so as not to push the stinger further into the body. Do not grab the stinger—this could squeeze the sac attached to the stinger and inject more of the venom.

- Wash the area of the bite or sting with soap and water to help reduce the chances of infection and to remove traces of the venom.
- Remove any jewelry from any bitten extremities because swelling is likely to occur.
- In most cases the reaction will be mild and localized. If possible, use ice or cold compresses on the site of the bite or sting. If the victim is bitten while directly conducting a surveillance, have him leave the site as soon as it is feasible to do so. Holding the bite area in a cool stream will likely help ease the pain, reduce the swelling, and slow the absorption of venom. Meat tenderizer may neutralize the venom, and calamine lotion can help to reduce the swelling if applied locally.
- If there is a more serious reaction, such as severe and rapid swelling or allergic symptoms, treat the bite just as you would a snake bite by applying constricting bands above and below the bite area. Be prepared to perform such basic lifesaving measures as rescue breathing. (This is why it is important to get EMT and other first-aid training for all members of the rural surveillance team.)
- Reassure the casualty and keep him as calm and comfortable as possible. If the reaction appears to be serious, evacuate the casualty and seek medical attention immediately.
- Remember that insect bites and stings can cause anaphylactic shock. This is a life-threatening situation, and if it appears that it is occurring you must immediately evacuate the casualty.

Prevention

There are a number of things you and your team members can do to prevent yourselves from being bitten.

- Use odorless insect repellant on all exposed skin areas and areas where insects might crawl on you, such as your ankles, wrists, head, and neck. Also spray areas where clothing will be tight against the body, such as the shoulders, to prevent insects from biting through.
- Reapply your repellant every few hours, especially if you are sweating a lot or it is rainy.
- Wear some type of insect netting over your head and neck. This will also aid in camouflage (but should not be your sole source of camouflage for the face and neck).
- Keep your uniform bloused to prevent insects from getting inside your clothing.
- If the situation allows wash daily or every few days, paying close attention to your groin and armpit areas.
- Use the buddy system to check each other for ticks and other insects.
- Wash your uniform if the situation allows and always bring a uniform change.

Tick Bites

These are something you have to be especially careful of while on a rural surveillance operation. Bites from some ticks can cause the transfer of a toxin into your system producing a fever most commonly known as Rocky Mountain spotted fever. It is important to frequently check yourself for ticks and to use the buddy system to check each other. On a number of operations I have had to force team members to check each other, but it is absolutely necessary.

First Aid

- Do not remove the tick by pulling it out.
- Apply the hot end of a lighted match to the body of the tick.
- Apply gasoline or turpentine to the head of the tick if the match doesn't work.
- Apply ice or cold compress to reduce absorption of toxin.
- Seek medical attention if any portion of the tick is left in the skin.

When assembling your field first-aid kit, be aware of the wide variety of emergencies you may encounter in a rural environment.

Snake Bites

There are approximately 130 varieties of nonpoisonous snakes in the United States. They can be identified by their oval-shaped heads and round eyes. While nonpoisonous snakes do not have fangs with which to inject venom, they can cause infection and may carry the bacterium that causes tetanus (lockjaw). In addition to that, they can scare the hell out of you. But if at all possible, you should avoid killing any nonpoisonous snake. Poisonous snakes are another matter. They are found throughout the world and throughout the United States. Some pot growers have been known to put them around their fields for the purpose of biting anyone who might venture into their growing area.

In the United States there are four kinds of poisonous snakes: rattlesnakes, copperheads, water moccasins, and coral

snakes. Rattlesnakes, copperheads, and water moccasins are called pit vipers because of the small, deep pits between the nostrils and eyes on each side of the head. They also have long, hollow fangs, thick bodies, slit-like pupils, and flat, triangular-shaped heads. In the event of a bite, there will be one or two fang marks along with a set of teeth marks on the victim.

A coral snake is different; it injects its venom through short, grooved fangs. The small coral snake found in the southeastern United States is brightly colored with bands of red, yellow, and black that completely encircle the body. The nonpoisonous scarlet snake and scarlet king snake have similar coloration in a different pattern; the thing to remember about identifying a coral snake is that the red ring always touches the yellow ring. You can remember it with the old rhyme "Red next to yellow can kill a fellow."

If you step on or otherwise disturb a snake it will almost always try to strike. Poisonous snakes do not always inject their venom when they strike; they may bite as a warning without injecting venom on the first strike. Even so, all snake bites are potentially dangerous because all snakes may have the tetanus bacterium in their mouths. Anyone bitten by a snake should seek medical attention whether the snake is poisonous or not. If you or your teammates are bitten, attempt to identify the snake and kill it if possible for the purpose of identification. This is important, because medical treatment will vary according to the type of venom. Treat all snakebites as poisonous if there is any doubt.

First Aid

Get the victim of a venomous snakebite to a medical treatment facility as soon as possible. Until evacuation or treatment is possible, have him lie quietly and not move any more than is absolutely necessary. He should not eat, drink, or smoke. If he has been bitten on an extremity, ensure that the extremity is kept level with the body. *Do not* elevate the limb! Keep him calm and try to reassure him.

If the bite is on an arm or leg, place a constricting band one or two finger widths above and below the bite. However, if only one constricting band is available, place that band on the extremity between the bite and the casualty's heart. If the bite is on the hand or foot, place the band on the wrist or ankle. The band should be tight enough to stop the flow of blood near the skin, but not tight enough to interfere with the circulation. If no swelling is present the bands should be placed about 1 inch from the bite. If swelling is present, put the bands on the unswollen part at the edge of the swelling. Keep a close eye on the bite site and if the swelling expands to or beyond the band, move it to the new edge of the swelling. (If possible, leave the old band on until you place the new one on the new

edge of the swelling, and then remove and save the old band in case the process must be repeated). If possible, place an ice bag on the area of the bite but *do not* wrap the limb in ice or place ice directly on the skin. *Do not* stop to get ice if it will delay evacuation or getting medical treatment.

Important: *Do not attempt to cut open the bite or suck venom out of the wound. If venom should seep through any damaged or lacerated tissues in your mouth, you will be poisoned as well.*

If a splint is used to immobilize the arm or leg, take extreme caution to ensure that the splinting is done correctly and does not bind. Check it frequently to see if it needs to be adjusted due to swelling.

When possible, clean the area of the bite with soap and water. Do not use ointments of any kind on the bite. Always remove rings, watches, or other jewelry from the affected limb.

Prevention

- Keep your hands off rock ledges where snakes are likely to be sunning themselves.
- Look around carefully before sitting down, particularly in deep grass among rocks.
- Attempt to camp on clean, level ground. Avoid camping near piles of brush, rock, or other debris.
- Check the other sides of large rocks before stepping over them.
- Avoid walking close to rock walls or similar areas where snakes may be hiding.
- Avoid hiking alone in a snake-infested area. It is important to have a companion to perform lifesaving first-aid measures and kill the snake.
- Handle freshly killed venomous snakes only with a long tool or stick. Snakes can inflict bites even after death by a reflex action.
- Wear heavy boots and clothing to provide some protection from snakebite.
- Be aware of the types of conditions where snakes thrive: brush, piles of trash, rocks, logs, and dense underbrush.

- Remember that all species of snakes can swim and can remain under water for long periods. A bite sustained in water can be just as dangerous as one received on land.

Human and Other Animal Bites

Due to the nature of rural surveillance, it is possible that an animal may bite you. This could be by a two-legged animal as well as a four-legged animal.

The human mouth is full of bacteria. If you or one of you team members is bitten by another human it is imperative that the bite be examined and treated as soon as possible. I have had medical personnel tell me they would rather be bitten by a dog than by another human because of the chance of infection from a human being's bite.

Animal bites can result in both infection and disease. Tetanus, rabies, and various types of fever can follow an untreated animal bite. Due to the complications that can follow, the animal that caused the bite should be captured or killed if at all possible. It is important not to damage the animal's head so that competent medical personnel can examine it to determine if it is carrying diseases. If you are unable to capture or kill the animal, provide medical personnel with any information that helps to identify it. This will aid in providing the appropriate treatment.

Bats, skunks, raccoons, foxes, dogs, and other wild animals may carry the viral disease rabies. Rabies is an acute infectious disease that affects the nervous system, primarily the brain. The incubation period in humans is normally 10 – 60 days. Symptoms from this may be depression, anxiety, and pain at the site of the bite. Acute symptoms may be difficulty in swallowing, salivation, muscle spasms, uncontrolled fear, and convulsions.

First Aid
- Cleanse the wound thoroughly with soap and water.

- Flush it well with water.
- Cover it with a sterile dressing.
- Immobilize injured arms or legs.
- Evacuate the victim immediately to a medical treatment facility.

CLIMATE

Owing to the nature of rural surveillance operations, it is not always possible to allow team members the time to adjust to being outside for extended periods. An individual's physical condition will determine the amount of time it takes to adjust to the climate, and this is why it is so important for team members to stay in reasonably good shape. Even those in good physical condition need some time to adjust to a hot or cold environment. Climate-related injuries are usually preventable, and it is important to recognize that prevention is both an individual and leadership responsibility.

There are a number of factors that contribute to the health and well-being of rural surveillance team members. Diet is a key factor, and the person's diet should be suited to his individual needs. If you are going to have a special diet determined by the climate, it should be adopted under appropriate supervision and must be properly balanced. Team members and leaders also need to ensure that everyone on a surveillance mission is getting enough sleep and rest.

Suitable clothing is vital to preventing climat-caused injuries. Clothing and gear that is specialized for surveillance can sometimes contribute to the problems of adjusting to a particular climate. Rural surveillance operators should use caution and judgement in adding or removing too much protective gear and clothing. You should be prepared to carry and return with all the gear you take in on surveillance. As a personal comment, I would rather take one or two things I didn't need than get out in the woods for a few days and not have something I really needed.

Heat Injuries

To prevent injury from exposure to extreme heat you need to drink adequate amounts of water. Every time a team stops its members should all drink some water if it is feasible; team leaders need to make each person drink water or other fluids frequently. Another factor in heat injury is activity level. Teams may try to move too fast to the target, and this can lead to overheating. Remember, stealth is more important than speed. It is also important to identify anyone on the team who may be especially prone to heat injuries such as someone overweight or who has suffered a heat injury in the past.

A balanced diet usually provides enough salt for the average person even in hot weather. Do not use salt tablets to supplement a diet. Anyone who is on a special diet should ask his doctor before adjusting his diet for a rural surveillance operation. Vitamin supplements are good but should not be used to replace a normal diet.

The mission and the climate are going to dictate the type of clothing and equipment each person is wearing. Wearing too much clothing or clothing that is tight-fitting is more likely to bring on a heat-related injury. Also, carrying a lot of equipment could also bring on these injuries if frequent rests stops aren't made. Whenever possible, it is a good idea to remove some equipment to allow for more ventilation and cooling.

Prevention

The ideal fluid replacement is water. Any time your team members have a chance to take in water they should do it, especially if they are moving. If the situation allows for it, you should get water each time you pass a water source. The body depends on water to cool itself and you can lose more than a quart of water through sweat per hour. In extremely hot climates the body will cool itself by sweating, and for the sweating to continue the body must have this water replaced. When the temperature is high and you are sweating a lot, try to drink at least a canteen of water every half-hour.

Keep in mind that as you sweat you are also losing minerals and these will need to be replaced as well. Remember that a person who has suffered a heat-related injury in the past is prone to another one. Other conditions that may increase heat stress and cause heat injuries include infection, being overweight, dehydration, exertion, fatigue, heavy meals, and alcohol.

Heat injuries can be divided into the categories of heat cramps, heat exhaustion, and heat stroke.

Heat cramps are caused by an imbalance of chemicals (electrolytes) in the body as a result of excessive sweating. Signs and symptoms are:

- Muscle cramps in the arms and legs
- Stomach cramps
- Excessive sweating
- Thirst

Treatment for heat cramps include the following:

- Move the individual to a cool or shady area
- Have him slowly drink at least a quart of cool water
- Loosen his clothing
- Seek medical attention if the cramps continue

Heat exhaustion is caused by a loss of water through sweating without adequately replacing the fluids lost. This can happen to the fittest individuals when they exert themselves in a hot environment. Signs and symptoms are:

- Headache
- Weakness
- Dizziness
- Loss of appetite
- Heavy sweating with pale, moist, cool skin

- Chills
- Heat cramps
- Nausea with or without vomiting
- Urge to defecate
- Confusion
- Rapid breathing
- Tingling in the hands and/or feet

Treatment for heat exhaustion includes:

- Move the patient to a cool shady location.
- Loosen or remove clothing.
- Pour water on him and fan him.
- Have him drink at least a quart of cool water.
- Elevate his legs.
- Have him avoid strenuous activity for at least 24 hours.
- Monitor the patient until symptoms are gone.
- Evacuate him and seek medical attention.

Heat stroke is caused by working in a hot, humid environment for an extended period. This can occur even when movement is limited, such as in a rural surveillance situation. Heat stroke is caused by the body failing to adequately cool itself. Inadequate sweating is a factor. *Heat stroke is a medical emergency and can result in death if treatment is delayed!* Signs and symptoms are:

- Weakness
- Dizziness
- Confusion
- Headaches
- Nausea and stomach pains
- Rapid and weak pulse and respiration
- Seizures

Treatment for heat stroke includes:

- Cool the casualty immediately.
- Move him to a cool, shaded area.
- Loosen or remove his clothing.
- Spray or pour water on him.
- Fan him to cool him and aid in evaporation.

- Massage his extremities.
- Elevate his legs.
- Have him slowly drink at least a quart of water.
- Continue cooling him until he receives medical aid.
- Continue to monitor for conditions that may require basic life-saving measures such as clearing the airway, mouth-to-mouth resuscitation, shock prevention, and bleeding control.

Cold Injuries

The very nature of rural surveillance requires that you lie still for long periods on the ground, the very activity that can bring on a cold injury.

Like heat injuries, cold injuries can also lead to serious problems and can compromise a rural surveillance operation. These injuries are most likely to occur when someone is unprepared and becomes exposed to cold temperatures. Cold injuries can usually be prevented through the correct use of protective clothing, personal hygiene, exercise, and proper care of the feet and hands. Air temperature, wind, precipitation, and even humidity can modify the loss of body heat. Low temperatures and dry cold can cause frostbite to exposed skin. Wind chill can cause the rapid loss of body heat and quickly aggravate old cold injuries. A person who has suffered a previous cold injury is more likely to suffer cold injuries in the future. Some conditions that are likely to bring on a cold injury are:

- Standing or lying in water for extended periods of time
- Failing to maintain an adequate diet
- Going for periods without adequate rest
- Extended contact with the ground
- Not being able to take care of personal hygiene
- Staying in the cold without being warmed for long periods

Prevention

The best defense for you and your team members against the cold is to be prepared. You should wear several layers of loose clothing, because it will be important to moderate your clothing based upon how the air temperature fluctuates. This is important in reducing excessive perspiration, which can later result in chilling. It is much better for you to be slightly cold than to be too warm and become dehydrated. If you are going to be moving or if the temperature rises, you should remove a layer of clothing. (You can put the additional layer back as the situation dictates.) Make sure each item and layer of clothing is camouflaged and blends in with your surroundings. Most cold injuries result from people having too few clothes when the weather becomes colder, so it is important to prepare for weather changes if you are going to be in the field for more than a day. Wet clothing can contribute to the cold-injury process and can, in fact, speed up the process.

Being in good physical condition can help prevent cold injuries. Fatigue contributes to carelessness, lower heat production, apathy, and disregard for personal hygiene. Mental fatigue and fear also reduce the body's ability to warm itself and increases the chances of a cold injury. People tend to become careless about taking precautionary measures.

It is important that all team members be trained to recognize signs and symptoms of cold injuries. A cold injury can happen to someone before they realize it because the injured part may already be numb. Numbness, tingling, or the sensation of pins and needles in the affected area are typical of superficial cold injuries. Sometimes this can be relieved simply by rubbing the area or by moving around and generating some heat. Outward signs of a cold injury may be discoloration of the skin or redness that eventually becomes pale or waxy white. An injured hand or foot will feel cold to the touch. If the injury is a deep one, swelling may be evident.

First Aid

The treatment for a cold injury depends upon whether it is superficial or deep. A superficial injury can be treated by warming the injured part by using body heat. You can put injured fingertips under your armpits or place your hands against your face to warm your cheeks. You can put your injured feet under the clothing and on the stomach of your buddy to warm them. (You need a good buddy for this!)

There are a lot of false remedies that do not work and can, in fact, cause great harm. Don't expose an injured part to a fire or stove; don't rub it with snow; don't soak it in cold water, and don't slap the injured area. Also, walking on feet that have a cold injury should be avoided if at all possible.

A deep cold injury such as frostbite requires more aggressive first aid. If not treated promptly and correctly it can lead to the loss of parts of the fingers or feet. If a team member has a deep cold injury, you should remove him from the operation and seek medical attention immediately. Treating a deep cold injury is not something you put off. If your surveillance is taking place during cold weather, check your team members each time for clothing and cold injuries before they move to set up surveillance on a target!

Some of the major conditions caused by cold are chilblain, immersion foot (also known as trench foot), frostbite, snow blindness, dehydration, and hypothermia.

Chilblain is caused by repeated and prolonged exposure of bare skin to temperatures below 60 degrees Fahrenheit. The skin may be swollen, red, tender, hot, and itchy. If untreated it can lead to infection and ulcerated or bleeding lesions. The best treatment is to apply body heat and rewarm the affected area. The area should *not* be massaged or rubbed. To prevent chilblain wear protective cold weather gear and stay as dry as possible.

Immersion foot results from fairly long exposure of feet to wet conditions at temperatures from 50 to 32 degrees. Keeping your feet inactive while wearing wet or damp socks and boots can bring on this condition. Also, wearing your boots too tightly and impairing circulation can increase the likelihood of immersion foot. If this condition continues for an extended period the feet may swell to the point that blood vessels in the feet lose circulation.

Serious cases of immersion foot can lead to the loss of toes and portions of the foot. Initially, portions of the affected part of the foot become cold and numb. Following this stage, affected portions may feel hot and burning and shooting pains may begin. In later stages, the skin may be pale with a bluish cast and a decreased pulse. Latter stages will show blistering, swelling, heat, redness, bleeding, and eventually gangrene. Immediate treatment actions should be taken for immersion foot regardless of the stage it is in when discovered. The only way to properly treat this injury is to gradually warm the affected part by exposing it to warm air. It should not be exposed to extreme heat and should be elevated to relieve the swelling. Symptoms may persist for days or weeks after treatment, and medical attention should be sought for any significant immersion foot.

Prevention of immersion foot is pretty simple: good hygiene for the feet and avoiding prolonged exposure to dampness. I have been on operations where at least twice a day I made team members change their socks and dry their feet when we weren't moving or on a target. I know of an army sergeant who was going through Special Forces school and got immersion foot. When he took his boot off a large portion of his heel separated from his foot, exposing some of his foot muscle. Needless to say, he was immediately evacuated to the Fort Bragg hospital and did not return. Throughout history, immersion foot has

defeated armies when their enemies couldn't do so. You must make your fellow team members take care of themselves.

Frostbite is another dangerous cold-weather injury. It usually occurs when tissue is exposed to temperatures below freezing. Factors such as wind chill, duration of exposure, and adequacy of protection also play a part. It is important to know if members of your team have ever suffered from frostbite before, as they will be prone to a second attack. The most likely areas to be affected are the nose, ears, cheeks, chin, hands, feet, forehead, and wrists. Frostbite can either affect the surface areas or it can extend deeper below the skin. It is important to seek treatment for frostbite immediately. There are progressive signs to frostbite:

- Numbness in the affected part of the body
- Sudden whitening of the skin followed by a tingling sensation
- Redness or grayish coloring of the skin (depending on the individual's skin coloring)
- Blistering
- Swelling or tenderness
- Loss of a previous sensation of pain in affected area
- Pale, yellowish, waxy-looking skin
- Frozen tissue that feels solid

Deep frostbite is a very serious injury and requires immediate medical attention.

Snow blindness can occur when the eyes are affected by glare from snow or ice. It usually occurs during an overcast or hazy day. On bright days the glare of the sun off snow or ice will cause a person to protect his eyes; however, on cloudy days people don't take the same precautions and the eyes are exposed longer to glare. They wait until discomfort is felt before taking steps to protect their eyes. Snow blindness may give the sensation of having grit in the eyes with pain in and around the eyes. There may be watering, redness, headache, and pain due to exposure to light. Conditions that cause sunburn may also lead to snow blindness. The best prevention is to use protective eyewear, not only as protection but to stop further injury. In an emergency situation it is possible to make field-expedient eyewear by cutting slits in wood or cardboard to allow the minimum amount of exposure to sunlight.

To treat snow blindness complete rest of the eyes is required. They should be protected from exposure to light with dark glasses and covering whenever possible. Snow blindness usually heals in a few days without permanent damage.

Dehydration occurs when the body loses too much fluid, salt, and minerals. Normal eating and drinking habits maintain the required levels of these fluids and minerals, but when an individual is involved in strenuous activity for an extended time, an excessive amount of fluids and salts are lost through sweating. If these losses aren't replaced, dehydration occurs. Simply making sure that fluid and mineral intake increases as activity increases can prevent this.

Dehydration occurs just as easily in cold climates as it does in warm climates. In fact, in cold environments it often goes unnoticed because people do not realize how much body fluid they are losing in contrast to what they feel in warm climates. Contrary to popular belief, dehydration in cold weather is a very serious threat because drinking to replace fluids in cold weather is often inconvenient, and sweat either evaporates or is absorbed into clothing before an individual notices how much he is sweating. Rural surveillance operators need to be aware that dehydration can incapacitate a member for hours, if not days.

If a team member experiences dehydration, some of the signs he will exhibit are difficulty swallowing and a dry mouth, tongue, and throat. He may also suffer from nausea, vomiting, dizziness, and fainting. He may have trouble focusing and feel tired and generally weak. If he begins to experience these signs, he should immediately be taken off the surveillance and kept warm and sheltered from the wind and cold so that he can rest and take in plenty of fluids. Medical treatment is critical, and he should be evacuated as soon as possible.

Hypothermia is the general cooling of the body. This condition is of particular concern to me, having once been a victim of hypothermia. Another soldier and I were on a field maneuver one winter and had been moving through the woods for about 36 hours. At about 3 A.M. we realized we were becoming disoriented and could not think straight. We also realized that we were probably suffering the early signs of hypothermia, so we stopped and got into a sleeping bag together to warm each other. After about two hours we were back to normal and were able to continue moving. We were very lucky; it could have been much more serious but we were in good shape, recognized what was happening to us, and took immediate action. Hypothermia has the potential to kill quickly. Cold and exhaustion can affect the body systems without notice. You do not need to be in freezing weather for this to occur.

As the body cools there may be signs such as progressive discomfort and impairment. There may be only a faint pulse or no pulse and shivering may occur as the body attempts to warm itself. A person may also become drowsy and his mental capacity can rapidly diminish. He will become disoriented, his speech may be slurred, and he may lose his coordination. As his body temperature continues to drop he can go into shock, his eyes become glassy, and his breathing shallow. Extremities may freeze and his core body temperature continues to drop leading to an irregular heartbeat or death.

The best way to prevent hypothermia is to do everything possible to avoid the rapid loss of body heat. A proper diet and adequate rest go a long way to prevent this. Also, being properly dressed and equipped for the environment is critical. Avoid working in wet clothing or remaining in wet clothing following a stream or river crossing.

Except for extreme cases of hypothermia, the best treatment is to evenly warm the person's body as soon as possible. This can be done in the field by using a campfire, sleeping bag, or the heat from another person's body. A hypothermia victim is unable to generate his own heat, so just putting him in warm, dry clothes, or a sleeping bag is not sufficient treatment. The drop of body temperature to 90 degrees or below, a weak pulse, coma, or unconsciousness indicate extreme cases. Always call for help and evacuate the person immediately to the nearest medical facility. Efforts to warm the casualty should be undertaken while he is awaiting evacuation. If his breathing stops, mouth-to-mouth resuscitation should be started immediately. If the casualty is conscious, warm liquids should be slowly given to him. Remember that hypothermia can come on suddenly and can kill quickly; it is a medical emergency and prompt medical treatment is called for.

SPRAINS, STRAINS, AND BROKEN BONES

On any rural surveillance operation, whether it is for training or the real thing, it is very likely that there will be some minor injuries. Hopefully you will avoid any serious injuries, but be prepared for some bumps and bruises.

Sprains and strains are the result of an excessive stretch or sudden force in the structures around a joint. This causes a pulling or jerking effect on these structures that leads to tears and bleeding. When this

happens, one or more of the following may be present:

- A history of previous injury to the area
- Swelling, redness, or muscle spasm
- Loss of some or all function
- Pain in the joint made worse by movement

When a sprain or strain occurs the best treatment is to follow the acronym RICE: rest, ice, compression, elevation.

Rest the affected area. Avoid any weight-bearing activity, protect the area from stress, avoid use using a splint if not needed.

Use ice with cold packs to shrink blood vessels in the area of the injury. Apply cold packs 20 – 30 minutes on/20 – 30 minutes off for the first 24 hours; wrap the cold pack to avoid direct contact with the skin.

Apply compression. Use elastic bandages to decrease swelling and give support.

Elevate the affected area. Raise the injury to a level higher than the heart to reduce swelling and pain.

Dislocations can take place as the result of a fall or exertion. When this occurs there will likely be intense pain, numbness, and an inability to move the affected area. There may be a weak pulse away from the injury and delayed capillary refill time. There will likely be an obvious deformity and a difference in the length of the extremities. The treatment is as follows:

- Immobilize the joint with a splint in a position of comfort.
- Elevate it if possible.
- Check for pulses.
- Apply ice for pain and swelling.
- Arrange for medical evacuation.
- Do not allow the casualty to eat or drink.

Fractures are breaks in the bone usually caused by a significant force to the bone. A closed or simple fracture is when the skin is intact. An open or compound fracture is when the skin is broken and the bone is protruding. Basic treatment is as follows:

- Splint the affected area in position; do not try to shift the bone.
- Immobilize the joints above and below the injury.
- Elevate the affected area to reduce swelling, blood loss, and pain.
- Cover an open fracture with a clean bandage.
- Arrange for medical evacuation.
- Do not allow the casualty to eat or drink.

POISON IVY, POISON OAK, AND SUMAC

Rashes from contact with poison ivy or poison sumac are a form of dermatitis and are caused by an allergic reaction to the oils of poison ivy, poison oak, or poison sumac plants.

Poison ivy can be found in every region of the United States except the Southwest, Hawaii, and Alaska. It appears as a weed with three shiny leaves and a red stem. (Leaves of three, let it be!) It also grows as a vine up trees or along riverbanks.

Poison oak is primarily found on the West Coast. It grows in the form of a shrub and has three leaves similar to those of poison ivy.

Poison sumac grows abundantly along the Mississippi River, but is far less common in other regions. It grows as a shrub and each stem contains seven to 13 leaves arranged in pairs.

The rash is spread by the oils touching parts of the body, not by the spread of the fluid from the blisters as is commonly thought. It is not contagious unless some of the oil remains on the skin and is touched by another person. The symptoms are as follows:

- Rashes usually appear within 1 to 3 days following exposure, although they may take as long as three weeks to appear. The worst stage is 4 to 7 days following exposure.

- Rashes may last 1 to 2 weeks.
- Redness and extreme itching are the first signs.
- Rashes may be in form of streaks or patches.
- Red pimples may form large, weeping blisters.
- Reactions vary from mild to very severe.
- Patients who are very sensitive may sometimes require hospitalization.

You need to seek medical assistance for someone who has an allergic reaction if the following occur:

- The rash covers more than a quarter of the body.
- There is swelling and/or difficulty breathing.
- The victim has had severe reactions to past exposure.
- The victim is coughing following exposure to smoke from burning plants.
- Itching is severe and cannot be controlled.
- The rash affects the face, lips, eyes, or genitals.
- The rash shows signs of infection such as pus or yellow fluid leaking from blisters.

First Aid
- Wash skin with soap and water as soon as possible following contact.
- Wash clothing and shoes with soap and water.
- Use calamine lotion to decrease itching.
- Apply 1 percent hydrocortisone four times a day for inflammation.
- For extreme conditions see a physician for oral steroids.

FOOT CARE

Foot care is essential for anyone involved in rural surveillance operations. Nothing can make a person useless in a field operation quicker than foot problems.

To avoid problems, foot hygiene is critical. As obvious and reasonable as it sounds, people often go to the field and fail to properly care for their feet. It is important to wash and thoroughly dry your feet, especially between the toes. Some people perspire more than others, and this includes their feet; they need to apply a foot powder at least twice a day. (If you are using foot powder, be sure you aren't also using boots that have Gore-Tex material. The foot powder will get into the pores of the Gore-Tex material and destroy the material's ability to "breathe.")

Properly fitting boots are critical. Many times people select boots based on how they look as opposed to how they fit. This is ridiculous, but it happens all the time. When selecting the boots you are going to take to the field you should ensure that they are comfortable, aren't too tight, and don't have pressure spots that hurt your feet.

It is also important to have several pairs of good socks. They should be the right size, padded, and clean. Always have clean socks to wear and wash them as often as possible if in the field for an extended period. If you do develop any foot problems such as blisters or fungus infections, make sure you treat them immediately. Left untreated, what starts as a minor foot problem can turn into a medical emergency overnight.

Make sure that footgear is properly broken in before you go on an operation. This can be accomplished on a training exercise, but never on a real operation. It's a good idea to have at least two pairs of broken-in boots at all times. It may save you a lot of foot problems and keep you from being evacuated during a real surveillance operation.

Chapter Four: Basic Fieldcraft

In almost any rural surveillance operation, the amount of time spent in the field observing the target will be dictated by the nature of the mission, the location of the target, and the risks involved. Some operations may last just a few hours, while others may go on for days or even weeks. However long the operation lasts, it is important that everyone is knowledgeable in some of the basics of survival and fieldcraft techniques. This will not only make their time in the outdoors easier, it may save their lives if they find themselves in a survival situation. Even the most experienced outdoorsman can become lost from time to time and may find himself having to use fieldcraft skills to survive. This chapter is by no means designed to cover all aspects of fieldcraft or survival but it does cover some of the fundamentals.

FIRE BUILDING

You may find yourself in a situation where you don't have matches or dry wood and staying warm may mean staying alive. On a rural surveillance you probably aren't going to have a fire even in your base camp, but there are situations where you might need a fire. The importance of a fire in a survival situation cannot be overemphasized. You need a fire for warmth, to keep you dry, for cooking, for boiling water, and for emergency signaling. In a survival situation your survival time may increase or decrease based on your ability to build and sustain a fire when needed.

When operating in a rural area you should always carry a supply of matches in a waterproof container. You need to practice shielding a match in a fairly strong wind. You should also know how to select and prepare a fire site, gather fuel, set the fire up, and light and maintain a fire using both natural and man-made materials. Remember that your life or the lives of your teammates may depend on your fire-building skills.

When building a fire, be sure to construct a firewall to prevent it from spreading. Make sure the rocks you use are not wet or porous; porous rocks can explode when heated, and if they hit you it's like shrapnel and can cause serious injury.

There are also some materials that should not be used as fuel in a fire. Fir, for example, can produce small explosions of sparks, which can cause the fire to get out of control. Bamboo, which grows all over the world, shouldn't be used because stalks burned in a fire will explode and can cause injury. Green bamboo and holly will give off dangerous gases when burned.

When preparing a fire in a rural setting, it is important to take extra precautions to avoid injury. Whether you are cutting wood and preparing tinder for a fire or starting the fire, do not get in such a hurry that you become careless.

Selecting a Site

When you decide to build a fire, try to select a site that has dry, mineral soil and plenty of wood (fuel) nearby. You shouldn't be running all over looking for wood and leaving the fire unattended. Also make sure you place the fire site in a spot that is suitable in relation to the shelter you will be using. To prepare the site, clear away dry brush and scrape the surface soil from the site. The cleared area should be approximately 3 feet in diameter to prevent the fire from spreading out of control. If available, use rocks or logs to construct a firewall to reduce flying sparks and block the wind from blowing on the base of the fire. The amount and direction of the wind will determine how you build the firewall. You may want to leave part of the wall open to allow for good ventilation.

If you find yourself in a situation where the ground is wet or covered with snow, you can make a firebase by laying several green logs side by side and building a fire on top of them. It is best to make two layers of logs, placing the second layer at 90 degrees to the first set of logs.

Fuel

You can categorize the fuels for your fire into three types. The order they should be used in is tinder, kindling, and sustaining fuel. Tinder is a dry material that will be ignited with a minimum amount of effort, even by a spark. Kindling is a readily combustible fuel that can be added as soon as the tinder produces a flame large enough to ignite it. Kindling is used to increase the temperature of the fire so that it will be able to ignite larger, less combustible material. The sustaining fuel is material that will burn slowly and longer than tinder or kindling. Large branches or logs are good for sustaining fuel.

Keep in mind that unless it has been dry for several days, you shouldn't collect tinder or kindling from the ground, since it will likely be too wet to start a fire with. Also, wood collected in the early morning hours will be damp from dew. You can collect dry hardwood from most any bush or branch by breaking off the dead ends. If you are in a tropical area during the rainy season, you can usually find good kindling on the inside of larger trees that often have hollow trunks. Also, dry deadwood may be found hanging in a network of vines. Driftwood from a seashore or river makes good sustaining fuel when allowed to dry out.

Laying a Fire

There are several ways to construct a fire lay. Keep in mind that good tinder in a sufficient amount is critical in starting a fire.

Cone

This is a technique where the tinder and a few sticks of kindling are put together in the shape of a cone with the fire starting in the center. As the core of this burns away, the outside kindling will fall inward, constantly feeding the heart of the fire. It is important that you do not put too much kindling on the outside until the fire begins to become established. This type of fire will radiate heat evenly and will burn well even with some wet wood.

Lean-to

By pushing a green stick into the ground at a 30-degree angle you can create a lean-to type of structure for a fire. If the wind is present, the top of the stick should point into the direction of the wind. Place at least a handful of tinder under the stick and place pieces of kindling against it. Light the tinder to ignite the kindling. As the fire increases, add more kindling until the fire is the size you desire or until you can start adding sustaining fuel.

Pyramid

To form this fire lay, place two small logs or large branches parallel on the ground. Place a solid layer of smaller branches or logs across the parallel logs. Add three or four more layers of branches, placing each layer vertical to the previous layer. As you build this up, each layer should be constructed smaller than the layer below it. After placing tinder and kindling on top, start the tinder and the fire will burn down into the branches and logs below. Since the fire burns downward, it burns evenly all around and requires little or no attention for some time.

Cross-ditch

Scratch a small cross in the ground about 1 foot across and 3 inches deep. (This is one of

Always pack a personal survival kit and take it with you no matter how long or short you think the operation is going to be.

the reasons you want to always take a good, small digging tool to the field with you.) Put a large wad of tinder in the center of the cross and build a kindling pyramid above the tinder. The shallow ditch will provide channels for the air to sweep under your fire, creating a draft to the fuel.

Fire stick

The fire stick is constructed by placing two rocks or two thick sticks on the ground about 10 inches to a foot apart. Lay the fire stick across the two sticks or rocks and place a large handful of tinder under the fire stick. Lean kindling on one side of the fire stick and light the tinder.

One of the most common mistakes made when trying to construct a fire is in the initial setup. Many people set the twigs so that the kindling collapses just when the tinder starts to burn out. If sustaining fuel is put on before the kindling has a chance to really start burning, it will smother the fire.

Starting a fire is often the biggest challenge you will face. Fires can be started in a number of ways either by using man-made materials and devices or by improvised techniques. Some man-made devices may include matches, cigarette lighters, metal matches, batteries, flares, pyrotechnics, or a magnifying glass. You might also use a type of man-made fuel to assist you but you should use caution if these are employed.

Improvised techniques may include a bow and drill or some other technique you are familiar with. Whatever technique you decide to use, be sure to take the precaution to shield your flame and fuel from the wind. Remember that there is always the potential for injury whenever you try to start a fire. Also keep in mind that unless it's a matter of survival, you do not want to have a fire on a rural surveillance operation. If you are the team leader or a member of a team that may operate in a rural environment, it is imperative that you practice the skills mentioned in this chapter. Like any other skill, if you don't practice fieldcraft and stay proficient you might not have the skill when you really need it.

SURVIVAL PLANNING

Survival planning is another area that all team members need to address because no one is immune from suddenly finding himself in a survival situation. It is a good idea to make it a team policy that each member of the team has his own survival kit with him at all times in the field.

Planning and training are the most important things you can do to prepare for a survival situation. The terrain will drive much of the type of training you will conduct. For example, if you operate in a mountainous region, you will train in how to safely move in that particular terrain. If you are going to be in a desert or arid environment, you will train in how to find and conserve water. One important part of this planning is to make sure that all of your shots, particularly tetanus, are up to date and that your dental work is taken care of. Although these may sound like small things, they can become life-threatening issues if you are out in a rural environment for any amount of time.

There is no shortage of survival kits you can buy on the commercial market. Some are pretty good; most are expensive. You can go to a store and construct your own survival kit for a fraction of what you would pay in most camping stores, and you can tailor it to meet your needs. But before you do that think about what you think you need to bring. Here's a list of basics to get you started. You will likely think of some things that I failed to think of. Remember that this kit is for your survival, so really give it some thought and also remember you have to carry it with you wherever you go, so think about weight and bulk.

- Insect head net
- Magnetic compass (backup)
- First-aid kit (backup)
- Pocket knife

- Signal mirror
- Water purification tablets
- Plastic eating utensils
- Box of waterproof matches
- Food packets
- Reversible sun hat
- Insect repellant
- Tool kit
- Gloves
- Snare wire
- Compressed trioxane fuel
- Survival fishing kit
- Poncho and liner
- Survival manual
- Shovel
- Plastic whistle
- Padded socks
- Sewing kit
- An 8x8 - foot waterproof cover
- Backup prescription medicine

Always try to include items that can serve more than one purpose in the field. A good sewing kit may also serve as a fishing kit and can be used in some forms of first aid. Keep in mind that everything that goes into your kit must be practical and have a purpose. Don't go with the cheapest stuff you can find; remember, your life may depend on this kit and what's in it. Keep all the items of your survival kit in one container that will be easy to carry and keep it in a location where you can get to it quickly if you need to.

It's a good idea to put together two survival kits at the same time. That way if you misplace one you will have a backup. If you have misplaced your survival kit and are getting ready to go out on a rural surveillance operation or some other activity that takes you into the wilderness, you are not likely to stop and put together another kit. Keep one kit in your pack and the other in your car where you will be able to grab it at the last minute if needed.

Any kit that you construct should be in a water-resistant and camouflaged container. Plan and construct the kit as though your life and your team members' lives depended on it because that may very well become the case. Make your survival kit small enough that you can distribute it in the cargo pockets of your pants; that way if you are separated from the rest of your gear, you will still have the most important items.

WATER

Water procurement will be one of your major concerns in any survival situation, whether you are in a desert, jungle, or mountainous environment. The average person can survive for three weeks without food but can last only about three days without water. Our bodies are three-fourths water and we have to have a good supply of it daily to maintain our health and to survive. Under strenuous conditions of living in the wilderness, people require more water than under normal conditions. Many people have died from thirst when there were sources of water close at hand; knowing where to look for water and how to procure it can save your life in a survival situation.

Even when the temperature is a mild 68 degrees Fahrenheit, most people require two to three quarts of water a day. That's a lot of water in a survival situation when you think about it. In colder climates a person requires less water—about two quarts unless he is involved in strenuous activities. When the temperature is extremely high and a person is active, he loses as much as four quarts of fluid a day. The body loses water in a number of ways in a survival situation through sweating, eating, breathing, urinating, and defecating. If a person is wounded or injured he could lose even more water.

A common mistake is trying to conserve water instead of trying to conserve sweat. The best way to conserve sweat is to keep physical activity to a minimum. This may not always be possible in a survival situation, but you should try. Being deliberate in all your activities, taking frequent rests, and working only during the cooler hours of the day or in the evening will go a long way toward conserving your water.

Wearing light-colored clothing (which you probably won't have on a rural surveillance operation) helps you to conserve fluids. Wearing some form of headgear also assists in conserving some water as well as protecting your head from the elements.

As mentioned in the chapter on first aid, thirst alone is not always a good way to determine your need for water or whether you may be getting dehydrated. You can operate in a cold environment and quickly become dehydrated. As a rule of thumb, you should take in enough fluids to put out at least a pint of urine every 24 hours. Urine that is dark or becoming dark is a sign that you are becoming dehydrated and you need to take steps to reverse the process. As a team leader in the field, I have made a point of reminding others to look to see if they were peeing darker and, if so, to drink more fluids. Don't feel silly doing this; it could save you and your team a lot of problems and possibly save someone's life. A team leader who fails to make sure his people have plenty of water and drink frequently isn't doing his job.

Losing just 5 percent of your body fluids can cause irritability, nausea, and weakness. Ten percent loss can bring on dizziness, headache, tingling in the limbs, and an inability to walk. With the loss of 15 percent of body fluids a person can experience dim vision, deafness, a swollen tongue, painful urination, and a numb feeling in the skin. The loss of more than 15 percent of bodily fluids may result in death. All of these are a good reason to make sure that you hydrate yourself frequently.

It is important to recognize the indicators of possible water sources around you, including:

- Drainages and low areas
- Large clumps of plush grass or other vegetation
- Animal trails
- Birds, ants, and bees
- Abundant vegetation

There are a number of methods of obtaining water in a survival situation. Many of them take time and experience and this book is about rural surveillance, not survival training. There are a number of excellent books on the market about survival and there are some that aren't so good. Get your hands on a good survival manual and make it part of your survival kit!

One of the best and easiest ways to procure water in a survival situation is through the collection of rainwater (if you are lucky enough to get rain). A poncho in your survival kit can be used to collect and drain the rainwater into a cup or canteen. If you can find a running stream you're in luck but make sure you have a good water filter and/or some water purification tablets. It is a good idea to hike upstream for a half-mile or more to see where the water is coming from—you don't want to get your drinking water from a stream running through a pasture where livestock are feeding.

There are several ways you can purify the water you collect. The most recognized and safest way is to boil the water. Water needs to boil for at least 10 minutes to ensure that you have destroyed all the harmful bacteria. Water purification tablets are also a good way to make your water safe to drink. You should make sure that an ample supply is part of your survival kit. Be sure to read the instructions and follow them carefully each time you use them. Iodine drops can also be used; tincture of iodine at 2 percent, with 5 drops added to your canteen of water, can kill most bacteria and make it drinkable. If the water is not clear you should add 10 drops of iodine and let it stand at least a half-hour before drinking. Adding 2 drops of bleach to a quart of water is another method for purifying water.

Remember that water is always one of your most immediate needs in a survival situation. Practice becoming proficient in different ways of finding, collecting, and purifying water in a rural setting. Your life may depend on it.

KNOTS

Whether constructing a shelter or building a litter to transport an injured person, a good working knowledge of ropes and knots can help you avoid many hardships in a survival situation. I once had an instructor in the army tell me that it's better to know six to eight basic knots than to try to learn how to tie and use all the knots there are and not know any of them well. This same instructor also said that the few knots you do know, you should be able to tie in total darkness. This has proven to be sound advice.

Understanding how to tie knots correctly is not something you can learn from a book. It is something you have to practice over and over until it becomes second nature and you can correctly tie them with your eyes closed and know they are tied the right way. I will discuss a few basic knots that can save your life in the wilderness. It is up to you to learn these knots and to practice them over and over again. You will need to know a little terminology to work with ropes. The *working end* of a rope is the end of the rope you are tying the knot with. The remainder of the rope is called the *standing end.*

Square knot
This one of the most basic knots. It can be used for a number of things, but primarily to tie two ropes of equal diameter together. If you have never tied a square knot or don't know what it is, take your time and slowly follow these steps. Form an overhand knot by placing the end of the left rope over and around the right rope just as you would when starting to tie your shoe. Place the rope on the right rope over and around the end of the left rope forming two interlocking loops. To secure this knot, tie a half hitch with the remaining ends of each rope.

Round turn with two half hitches
This is an anchor knot used when the rope is going to be under constant pressure. It is useful when you need to put in a rope that will assist others climbing up a steep hill. Always select a secure anchor, such as a well-rooted tree or a large solid rock when using this knot. With the working end of the rope wrap it around your anchor. Bring the working end of

the rope back over the standing end of the rope and then back under to form a half hitch. Do this again to form a second half hitch in the rope. This knot, tied properly, will support as much weight as the rope will hold. It is a very simple knot with lots of uses and can be tied and untied very quickly.

Clove hitch

This is an intermediate anchor knot that can be tied in the middle or at the end of the rope. You can tie an end of the rope in a clove hitch by placing the working end over the anchor and then bringing it back under the anchor and over the top of the working end and back over the anchor again. Bring the working end back under the anchor a second time and take it over the anchor and under the second wrap of the rope that lies over the anchor. Pull the ends in opposite directions. This one sounds difficult but after you practice it a couple of times you will quickly get the hang of it.

Bowline

This is an anchor knot that has a number of uses and can come in handy if you need to use a basic knot to rescue or secure someone. To tie a bowline, form an underhand loop in the rope leaving sufficient rope on the working end to form the desired size of knot. Pull the end of the rope up through the loop and take it around the standing end of the rope. Pass the working end back through the loop again. This will form a loop. With your other hand, pull the standing end. With the remaining working end, form a half hitch around the loop of the bowline. If tied properly, this knot has a multitude of uses.

Prusik

This knot can be used on another rope of equal or greater diameters and can be locked in one position by using tension. One of the great things about a Prusik knot is that once the tension is released, the knot can be untied or quickly moved to another position on the other rope. To tie the Prusik knot into an anchor rope, form a loop in the middle of your rope and lay

it over the anchor rope. Place both ends of your rope under the anchor rope and run them through the loop you just laid over the anchor. Repeat this and then tie an overhand knot with the ends to form the knot.

Shears lashing

This can be used to tie poles together if you need to build a shelter. This is done by using poles of approximately the same size and tying a clove hitch to the first pole. Make two or three loose wraps around both poles and then wrapping the rope around itself several times. Finish this by tying a clove hitch to the second pole. This lashing will hold the poles together and yet will not form a knot you can't get untied at a later time.

These knots are basic and can help you in a survival situation. Practice using them so that when needed you can tie them the right way in total darkness.

WEAPONS AND TOOLS

Being in a survival situation is bad enough but finding yourself in a survival situation without your equipment or weapons is about as bad as it gets. Those who have survived such situations possessed imagination and ingenuity. You may need to either find or fashion a field-expedient weapon—anything from a club to a spear to a bow and arrows. If you constructed a good survival kit you will be able to fashion an assortment of weapons to protect yourself and to hunt game. A forest environment will provide you with an array of items you can use to construct a crude weapon. Sticks, stones, animal bones, and vines can support you in this effort. Just use your imagination and when you are planning your survival kit remember you may need to construct weapons.

SIGNALING

Signaling techniques have saved many people in survival situations. Had it not been for their signals, they likely would not have survived their ordeal. The first thing you should do in a survival situation, if at all possible, is establish communication with someone (unless you are in a hostile environment). It is important for you remember that it is extremely difficult to spot a person or even a group of people from the air. It is even more difficult when there is limited visibility. If there is a lot of foliage, it is near impossible.

On a rural surveillance operation, the foliage covering and protecting you can be your enemy if you are trying to signal someone to rescue you. You must be prepared to send a signal to rescuers that they can see and recognize as someone in need of help. If you are signaling an aircraft, the speed and altitude of that aircraft can work against you. If you don't use a signal that will catch the pilot or spotter's attention, you may not get a second chance. It is a good idea to have a signaling device or devices in your survival kit. It is critical to remember the following points when choosing your signal to best attract attention:

- A change in colors and shadows
- Man-made patterns such as triangles, circles, straight lines, and X's that do not occur in nature
- A flashlight at night
- A large fire and a lot of smoke
- Movement of a signal device that is large and bright (however, signal slowly, because a signal that is too fast will blur and not be noticed)

When you are making plans to signal for help, the basic things you must try to remember are (1) which signals you want to use, and (2) to have your signals ready to use on very short notice.

There are a number of items that you can use for signaling. Again, these are things you need to think about when planning and putting together your survival kit.

- Flashlights
- Mirrors
- Clothing
- Signal panels
- Strobe lights
- Pyrotechnics
- Smoke
- Fires
- Pen flares

If you are going to signal with fire, be sure to build it in the shape of a triangle—the international distress signal—or construct three fires in a straight line approximately 25 yards apart. It is important to lay your fires as soon as possible and protect them so they can be lit when you need them.

Also consider your location. If you are in an area thick with trees, remember that foliage can disperse smoke to the point that it won't be seen from the air; try to find a clearing where the smoke and, hopefully, the fire will be seen. If you are in an area with lots of snow on the ground, be sure to build your signal fire on a platform or rocks so that the melting snow won't put the fire out. Also, consider the background that the smoke will be seen against. White smoke against a snow-covered landscape will not be as visible as dark or black smoke. Adding an oil product such as rubber or oil-soaked rags to the flames can generate black smoke. Signaling with smoke is most effective when done on relatively calm days. High winds disperse the smoke too fast, and may send the fire out of control. You can purchase smoke grenades or other signaling devices designed to get a searcher's attention.

A flash from a mirror or flare is an excellent signaling device. When you use a signal mirror, try to aim the reflection toward the cockpit of the aircraft. Again, consider your environment. Fog or haze can obstruct the light reflecting off your mirror. If at all possible, signal from high ground even if it is only a few feet above the rest of the surrounding terrain. Under good conditions, a signal mirror has a range of 70 miles.

Flashlights can also be used to signal by sending an SOS signal—three dots, three dashes, three dots. Strobe lights also make excellent signaling devices and many are very effective, even during the day. But just as with flashlights, be sure to check your batteries before you leave home.

Signal panels are good to have, and many of the commercial models can also serve as temporary shelter. (However, if the panel is your primary signaling device, don't use it as your primary shelter, too.) Good signal panels can be used during daylight, with the orange side of the panel being the best to signal with. Just as with a flashlight, the signal panel will be easier to see from the air if you keep flashing it to create an eye-catching display. An orange panel 3 feet by 5 feet should be the minimum.

Another way to signal is to use articles of clothing that might be seen from a distance. It probably won't do a lot of good to wave a piece of clothing that blends in with your surroundings, but a bright piece of clothing that contrasts with the foliage may do the trick.

If you use ground signals to attract attention, be sure to arrange them in large, geometric patterns. In the snow, tramp out letters or symbols and fill in the empty spaces with twigs or branches. In sand, use rocks, vegetation, or seaweed to form a signal. If you are in an area that has lots of brush, cut out patterns in the vegetation or burn out the brush.

In a region that has tundra, try to dig trenches or turn the sod upside down to make a signal that can be seen from the air. Remember to always make the symbol in a geometric pattern big enough to be seen from a distance.

If you are signaling to a fixed-wing military aircraft and it sees your signal, the pilot should signal that the message is understood by rocking the wings from side to side during daylight or if there is a bright moon. He may also make green flashes with the starboard wingtip signal light during darkness. The pilot may signal that the message is not understood by making a complete circle to the right and/or by flashing his red signal light (a civilian aircraft doesn't have this signalling capability).

Remember to plan for signaling when packing for a rural surveillance operation in remote areas. Proper signaling is the quickest

way to ensure rescue and quick recovery. Your situation on the ground and the surrounding environment will determine the type of signaling you can use. A word of warning: If you are in an area where some of the people may be hostile to you, remember that the signal makes you more visible to them as well.

FINDING GAME

The preparation of fish and game may be necessary if you are in a survival situation for an extended period. It is not possible to fully prepare you for such a situation with one chapter. However, I do want to provide you with some points to remember if you need to live off the land for a while.

In a survival situation, fish may be the easiest game for you to catch. If so, the following points should be remembered.

- Gills should be red or pink in color. If the gills are grey or white the fish is spoiled and must not be eaten.
- The body should be wet or moist, not slimy.
- The scales should be a pronounced shade of gray, not faded.
- The eyes should be clear.
- Press your finger against the fish; if it remains dented it's probably stale.
- If the fish has a sharp or peppery taste don't eat it.
- Fish should be prepared as soon after catching as possible.
- All fish along the North Pacific coast are edible.
- The safest fish to eat in tropical areas are those caught beyond the reef. (Many fish in muddy or sandy shores have toxins in their skins.)
- Do not eat any fish eggs found in clusters on rocks, logs or reefs.
- Any fish longer than 4 inches should be gutted and scraped clean.

All reptiles can be eaten but many are dangerous; use caution when trying to catch one. Because they are cold-blooded, reptiles do not have the blood-borne diseases carried by warm-blooded animals. You still should use caution when preparing them, but in emergency situations they can be eaten raw. Whether it is a lizard, turtle, or snake, always use caution when catching a reptile. Even if a snake is not poisonous, its bite can become infected and cause serious health problems. The only exception to eating reptiles is that you should not eat box turtles; they consume poisonous mushrooms, and the toxins can be deposited in the meat of the animal.

Catching and preparing fowl and mammals can be challenging. Traps are your best bet.

When you trap game it is likely going to be alive when you check the trap; use extreme caution and kill the animal quickly and humanely. If you find dead animals that were not trapped by you, they probably have been dead for some time and may be diseased. Unless there is no other choice, leave them alone and move on. Any good survival manual has instructions on how to prepare wildlife for eating. I strongly suggest you pack one with your survival kit and read it.

Knowing the basics of fieldcraft will better prepare you for rural operations. Knowing what to do in an emergency situation will also prepare you for operations that end up lasting longer that you had planned.

Chapter Five:
Land Navigation
and Route Selection

One of the best ways I know to avoid finding yourself in a survival situation is to not get yourself into one in the first place. Most people put themselves in such a situation by getting lost. If you don't know how to navigate in the woods you shouldn't be there in the first place and you certainly shouldn't be trying to conduct a rural surveillance. Many times people have been lost for days as the result of going for a "short walk in the woods." On a rural surveillance operation, even if you are only traveling for a short distance to your target, you *must* understand map reading and land navigation.

MAPS

The first thing you need for rural surveillance is an accurate map of the area you will be operating in. Today's maps are prepared from photographs taken from an airplane; many older maps are updated by this method. It is critical when planning an operation that you have the newest maps available. If you have an older map to work and plan from, you must be conscious of this and be prepared to adjust to the fact that there may or may not be things in the area not reflected on the map itself. For high-risk operations, it is strongly advised to arrange for aerial photography of your target area.

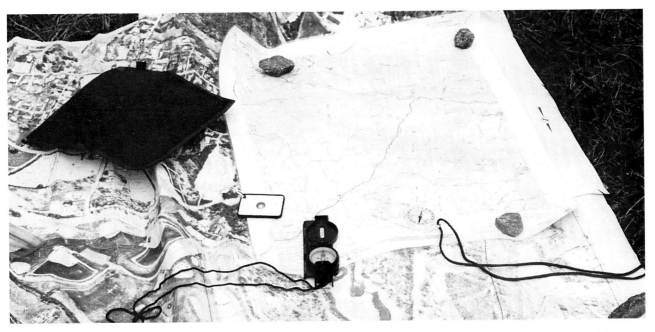

Water-resistant maps of the area (and the skill to read them properly) are vital navigational tools. Invest in a good-quality compass as well.

During your operational planning, as well as during the operation itself, you should take care to protect the maps you are using. You should never mark on any of them, including the ones you will leave behind at headquarters. Maps can reveal sensitive information about your activities to those who do not need to know. Likewise, maps you take to the field may become compromised. If they are found with notes and marks on them it could put your life and the lives of your team at risk. I always make a point of inspecting team members' maps before and during operations to make sure they aren't marked in a way that might compromise the mission. Operational maps should be considered sensitive documents and should not be allowed to be seen or fall into the hands of anyone not directly involved in the operation.

Also, great care should be taken to protect a map in the field by keeping it in a waterproof case or by covering it with a water-resistant plastic such as a sealable food storage bag.

Most people are familiar with city maps and road maps. A rural surveillance operation will likely also require the use of a topographical map, which depicts the elevation and terrain of an area. Since the features of the terrain cannot be shown on a map exactly as they exist in real life, shapes and colors are used. To read a topographic map you will need to know the following colors and symbols.

- *Black* represents man-made features such as buildings, roads, power lines, railroads, trails, and boundaries.
- *Red* depicts primary and secondary highways. Solid or dashed straight red lines indicate the lines of a survey that may belong to the U.S. Public Land Survey System.
- *Green* shows areas of vegetation. The shade of green may determine how dense the vegetation may be. This is often not reliable on maps more than a few years old. Open fields are often shown in white and woods or orchards may be designated by green dots.
- *Blue* areas and lines indicate water. An area

that is solid blue obviously represents a lake, reservoir, or ocean. Perennial streams are shown as thin, continuous lines. Rivers are thicker lines. If the line is dotted it means that the stream or river is intermittent. Swamps and marshes or also shown in blue with a symbol indicating a swamp or marsh.

- *Brown* is used to illustrate topographic features. Thin brown lines called contour lines provide a visual depiction of the terrain. Being able to read these lines is one of the keys to map-reading and land navigation.
- *Purple* is used to indicate features that are added to the map when it is revised. These changes to the original are usually as the result of an aerial reconnaissance.

Maps come in different sizes and scales, which can cause confusion, and it is important that all team members are working off the same maps with the same scale. The map scale is the numerical relationship between the distances and sizes depicted on the map and their actual distances and sizes. The scale of each map is depicted on its margin, usually at the bottom.

One of the things you must always remember when using a map in the field is to orient it to the terrain surrounding you. Since all maps are printed with the top of the map pointing north, use your compass to determine north and position your map where the top of the map is also north. If you know your location and you have oriented your map correctly, you will be able to observe the terrain around you in relation to how it is depicted on the map. Your map is oriented correctly when the details on the map correspond correctly to the features of the landscape around you. Orienting the map by using your compass and a main road or some other prominent terrain feature helps to ensure that you have oriented it properly. You can repeatedly reconcile that you have oriented the map properly by checking it with houses, fields, rivers, or other features depicted on the map.

Contour lines show the shape and elevation of the land you are traveling. A map with contour lines often shows a thicker reference contour line that indicates the elevation of that line. Contour lines are two-dimensional representations of three-dimensional objects such as hills or the slope of a valley. The contour interval is the distance between these brown lines, and they depict the difference in elevation between the lines. The contour interval used on a map is stated in the map's margin information.

If these lines are close together, there is a sharp difference in elevation and the slope of the terrain will be steep. If the space between these lines is more spread out then the slope of the land is gentle. When cliffs or steep embankments are depicted on a map by contour lines, the lines often run together. When there is a large field or forest that is almost level, the lines are very far apart. Understanding how these lines represent the lie of the ground is critical to planning your direction for movement in a rural surveillance operation.

Understanding and reading a map are critical to selecting routes for a rural surveillance operation. If you do a poor job of route selection, you may miss the target and could endanger your team and the entire operation. Selecting the routes to and from the target area can make the difference between success and failure. It is important to remember that unless the maps you are planning from are current and accurate, it is very likely that you are going to run into obstacles that will alter your original plan and may delay your movement. Allow for this in your planning. Vegetation is one thing that dramatically changes everything once you get on the ground and start moving. I recently was moving through an area to a bridge next to an open field. In reality, the map was years old and that open field had become an area filled with small trees and very thick undergrowth that made it almost impassable. As a result, I had to go a long way to finally get to where I wanted to be simply because I planned my route using an old map.

When you select a route to travel, remember to avoid roads and trails if at all possible. These provide little concealment for a team and make it easier for someone to locate and track you in these areas. Be aware that marshes, creeks, and riverbanks are often surrounded by thick vegetation and are difficult to travel. Also be aware there is a higher chance of exhaustion and injury when traveling in steep terrain.

It is most important that each team member has a reliable compass and knows how to use it. It is also a good idea to have a second compass as part of your survival kit. (I also recommend having a second map of the area in the survival kit.) I try to make a habit of having three compasses when I go on an operation. A compass is the primary navigation tool you will use on most rural surveillance operations. It is critical if you are tracking someone. There are several types of compasses; some are excellent while others are just pieces of junk. The military uses a lensatic compass that is both simple and accurate. Suunto makes excellent compasses, as does Silva. Some of these can be very expensive, and often the more expensive ones are not that good. A compass priced in the midrange will likely do as well as a more expensive one.

The arrow of the compass always points to magnetic north (the North Pole). But there are actually three "norths" in map reading. There is true north, magnetic north, and grid north. The difference of these "norths" is small in the eastern United States and will make little difference unless you are traveling great distances. For the purpose of rural surveillance it is not necessary to understand how to convert one reading to another. Being able to read the terrain and know your exact location also makes this conversion unnecessary. Your compass arrow points to magnetic north, and that is how you should orient your navigation. Since the floating needle in your compass is influenced by the magnetic pull of the North Pole it is important to remember that it can also be influenced by other magnetic items, so you should never take an azimuth reading with your compass held next to a metal object. Readings taken under power lines or across the hood of a vehicle can also cause the compass to give an inaccurate reading. Even resting your compass on top of your weapon can cause a false reading; if you do this continually it can take you and your team far off track.

The more often you and your team can get into a rural area and practice moving and navigating together, the better you will perform when you have an actual surveillance operation to perform. As you work and train together, you will learn who are the best navigators on your team just as you will learn who is the best point man, rear security, etc. This will also allow your team members to become more proficient in such skills as land navigation so that when necessary, they can relieve others. A big part of learning to read maps, recognize terrain features, and navigate across the land is doing it over and over through practical exercises. In training sessions, I have taken the weakest navigator and made him responsible for getting the team to an objective. Recently I was training a team and one of the members had no idea how maps and compasses worked. By the end of that week the guy was ready to take up orienteering!

You must rotate your compass man to other functions to ensure he doesn't get burnt out or too confident. In team training it is a good idea to set up a compass course for day and night training in an area your team mates are not familiar with. Set out some points or use prominent terrain features and require them to navigate to them as buddy teams. Make it a requirement that the weakest navigators have to do most of the compass work. If necessary, put them with someone who knows map reading and land navigation and who can help them improve. This is also a good way to maintain the skill of moving quietly and undetected through the woods. I have used a state park area filled with visitors and made it part of the training requirement to move without being observed by others and still find the next map point.

Land navigation training makes team members do terrain association while moving from point to point. Understanding map

contour lines becomes necessary and observing these lines on a map and the terrain gives a third dimension to these lines. Observing these lines quickly teaches how they represent the five major landforms (hilltops, valleys, ridges, saddles, and depressions). It is also helpful to lay out the map course where it takes the participants to high ground where they can see many of the terrain features.

Determining the best routes to take can often be tricky and is influenced by many variables. Factors such as the target and the threat you may be facing can determine what route you must take. The number of people and how much equipment you have to bring can also influence which routes you select. Once you have planned your routes, you will need to set the azimuths you follow for each leg of your movement.

An azimuth is defined as a horizontal angle measured clockwise from the north baseline. It sounds more complicated than it is. Actually it is just common sense. Imagine the face of a clock with 12 o'clock being north, or 0/360 degrees. East is 90 degrees (3 o'clock). South is 180 degrees (6 o'clock). And west is 270 degrees (9 o'clock). If you need to move on an azimuth of 45 degrees, you will be traveling northeast.

TERRAIN ASSOCIATION

Map reading and land navigation are things that you need to actually do and experience before you can really understand and appreciate them. That is why training as a team is so important before going on an actual operation. Terrain association is also something you need to do as a practical exercise before you can be proficient at land navigation.

For terrain association you need a clear understanding of contour lines on the map in relation to the actual terrain. By observing contour lines in detail, you should be able to imagine how the terrain actually lies. Features such as hilltops, slopes, saddles, depressions, and ridges should be seen in your mind as you view contour lines on a map. This is not something that can be developed quickly. It is a perishable skill that must be practiced if you are to stay proficient. By moving through rural terrain and observing the map and comparing it with the terrain features around you, you will be able to develop this skill. It also helps you to appreciate how vegetation can mask the terrain you are traveling through.

Comparing man-made features around your location with those on the map can be helpful and important when doing terrain association; however, it is important that you keep the age of the map in mind. Man-made objects can be added or removed after the map is drawn. I have found that it is best to rely on the natural features. A mountain that was there 15 years ago when the map was made is likely to still be there today. If you get confused from an old map, trust the natural features. They rarely change.

Another helpful tool when conducting terrain association during navigation is to use inland bodies of water. This is done by comparing the sizes and shapes of bodies of water such as lakes, ponds, and rivers to help you determine your location. The shapes and sizes of lakes as well as the sizes and the direction of flow of rivers and streams can aid with terrain association and land navigation.

Seasonal changes have a direct impact on terrain association. They also have a critical impact on route selection for a rural surveillance operation. This is particularly true in those areas where seasonal changes are distinct. An area that may offer good cover at one time may offer little or no cover during other seasons. Likewise, areas that may be difficult or almost impossible to pass through during one season can be easy to traverse during another.

During the winter, heavy snow can pack the vegetation down and delineate the lie of the land. I have seen heavy snow on top of the land and vegetation to the point that it actually shows the form of the land beneath it, causing the land to appear as though it showed the contour lines on the map. In the spring, foliage will grow back and conceal the landforms and make the terrain more difficult to recognize.

This effect usually lasts through the summer and into early fall.

During rainy season changes can occur that temporarily change the terrain. Also, erosion can make changes that modify the shape of the land. Over time these changes can be permanent and significant. Likewise, a long drought can change the shapes of lakes and sometimes even make streams disappear.

At the beginning of this chapter I stated that getting lost is one of the ways people find themselves in a survival situation. Getting lost is also a way to learn how to navigate in the woods. I'm proud to say that I personally have never been lost but I have been disoriented more times than I care to remember. Figuring my way out of these disorienting situations helped me to be a better navigator. In case you ever find yourself lost (or disoriented) there are several things you should remember.

- Remain calm.
- Sit down and take a break.
- Study your map and the area around you.
- Think about what you did and saw during the past few hours.
- Find the point on the map that you are certain was your last known location.
- Recall the objects/terrain features you passed since that location.
- Look for distinct features around you and compare them with features on your map.
- Keep your map oriented while you are comparing features.
- If you cannot backtrack to your last known position, find a large object on your map such as a river or highway. If it is to the west of what you believe is your general position, begin navigating toward that area observing the terrain and comparing it with your map as you move along.
- Use your compass and the terrain to avoid traveling in a circle.
- Remember that people who stay lost are those who panic and fail to think clearly.

Chapter Six:
Tactical Movement

Tactical movement could be defined as moving in such a way as to keep the team from being detected, and in such a way as to defend itself if it is detected and attacked by an enemy force. It is critical to the success or failure of the rural surveillance operation. Injury or worse can result if tactical movement isn't conducted correctly at all times. If you and your team let your guard down and stop moving tactically, that is the moment you will compromise yourself and the operation. In this chapter I cover the things I know to be

important for a good tactical movement. By no means do I cover every point that should or could be made regarding this subject. Someone else will have another good technique or idea I am not aware of or that I failed to mention. As I tell students when I teach rural surveillance, "These are things that work for me. They are not the gospel, and if you have a better way of moving tactically, by all means use what works best for you."

The more you work and train in something, the more proficient you and your team become.

Practice moving together until you move as one unit. Always remember to give yourself 360-degree coverage.

Maintain security at all times. When you stop, make sure all the vantage points are covered.

Learning and implementing tactical movement is critical to *any* part of a rural surveillance operation. Whether it involves moving to the general area of an operation, moving from a drop-off point to the target itself, or moving those last few hundred yards on to the target, good tactical movement ensures success.

If you are genuinely concerned about being a professional rural surveillance team, you must train together. This means getting out into a rural environment frequently and practicing moving together in a tactical manner. It is not the same as walking through the woods; it is hard work and it takes concentration and discipline. I can't tell you how many times I have seen "teams" throw things together and go out for a recon on a target when they haven't really worked together in the woods. It is a joke and results in nothing more than a group of men trying to tiptoe through the woods making an effort to be quiet. Tactical movement is more than just being quiet. It is a matter of remaining undetected and working together as a team, being prepared for anything that might happen while in the woods.

Assuming that you have taken care of all the things discussed earlier, such as good planning, selecting the right team members, acquiring and training with the right equipment, and conducting a thorough map reconnaissance, the challenging part is the tactical movement itself. The team members probably have a formation they prefer to move in and will use this most of the time they are out. Formations for movement are, of course, going to be dictated by the number of people, terrain, vegetation, and the situation. Other factors such as the weather, the threat, and the amount of equipment may dictate what type of formation you move in. I have my own preference, but as long as the formation you use ensures security coverage of 360 degrees, it should be sufficient.

This brings up security, a critical point, so let me address it now. Security for an actual rural surveillance operation begins at the time the decision to conduct the operation is made. I mention this here because all the good tactical movement in the world is not going to ensure a successful operation if the mission is

During training constantly review what's working and what isn't.

compromised. Never make the mistake of thinking that because you are secure when you are in the field that you have a secure operation. Operational security must be uncompromising, and it begins the moment the decision to conduct an operation is made.

PRINCIPLES

There are several basic principles you must practice when conducting tactical movement for a rural surveillance operation. First, it is imperative that you have team members who can navigate. As mentioned previously, all plans and preparations are useless if you can't get to your objective, and poor navigation puts the team at risk by exposing it to unknown areas needlessly. Also, depending on the size of your team, plan on having members back each other up by using several compass men and several pace men. Pace men count and keep track of the distance the team has traveled from one point to another so that it can be determined where they are on the map. If you have more than one person on these positions,

they can check each other to ensure that the team is moving to the target area the way it had been planned.

Any tactical movement must employ stealth to remain concealed. When planning the route you intend to take, remember to exploit the terrain to cover and conceal your team. Use rough, swampy, or heavily vegetated terrain to mask your movement. If possible, move when visibility is reduced, such as during darkness, fog, rain, or snow. Wind will also help you remain undetected because it masks much of the noise your movement might create. You can also avoid detection by moving at times when people are most likely to be sleeping or distracted. It is very helpful to know the habits of those in the area you are traveling; I have usually found it ideal to move when there is a moderate rain and wind, no moon, and at between one and five o'clock in the morning.

Constant security is critical during a tactical movement. From the moment you begin moving to the area until you have safely returned you must maintain security, which involves inconvenience, hard work, and, most of all, discipline. Maintaining security means everything from working as a team to maintain 360-degree security during movement as well as during all stops, to make certain that someone is on guard when other members of the team are resting. Light and noise discipline must be enforced at all times to ensure that the security and location of the team is maintained. A minimum amount of talking and movement must be enforced to prevent detection.

During tactical movement everyone must take both active and passive security measures at all times. Team members must be given responsibility for security enroute to the area, at danger areas, while in base camp, and while in observation sites on the target. If you don't ensure constant security, the entire team and the operation is in jeopardy.

When planning your tactical movement, consider using support personnel to assist you in remaining undetected. If you have a particularly difficult target, you may want to employ someone to create a distraction while you move through or into an area. This is something that must be carefully planned and coordinated and will be dictated by the situation. You are only limited by your imagination, but it is something to consider when working against a difficult target.

OVERLAND MOVEMENT

Regardless of how you get to the area of your target, you are most likely going to move on foot for the final legs of the operation. The movement formations and techniques you choose should be based on your location and what works best for the team. During daylight hours it is usually best to move in a modified column type of formation. It is vital to have your people dispersed as much as possible so that they can communicate visually with each other while at the same time covering their own areas of security. The terrain, vegetation, and weather will dictate how dispersed members can be and this will fluctuate as surroundings change.

As visibility is reduced, either as the result of weather or nightfall, you will likely be forced to change from a modified column to a line formation. I was recently on an operation with a team that started off just at dusk in a narrow modified column formation. In less than 20 minutes the team members were traveling in a very close file formation due to reduced light and increased vegetation. In just a few more minutes, they were in a tight line formation moving very slowly due to the fact there was no moon and no light. Each was literally maintaining contact by holding on to the man in front of him and traveling in almost total darkness. As a result, the team had to move very slowly and the operation took a lot longer than had been anticipated.

Your point man in any movement should be one of your sharpest and most experienced members. He is responsible for alerting the team to any approaching dangers and must communicate with the rest of the team at all times. This is a position that requires a lot of concentration. If the point man fails to be observant, the entire team and the operation could be compromised. The point man must also be able to navigate well and move quietly and undetected. It's hard work, and you should plan to have someone relieve the point man from time to time if possible.

It is a good idea to designate someone as the compass man and pace man to keep constantly checking the direction of movement and location of the team. Although the team leader should also do this, it is a good idea to have your most experienced navigator responsible for this duty. This person needs to be close to the team leader to advise him of the team's exact location.

Whether you travel in a modified column, a line, or some other formation, it is absolutely vital that all team members know which areas they are responsible for in regard to security. The team leader must periodically check that team members are clear about the area they should be watching as the team moves and as it stops. Failure to have 360-degree security is not an option. Many times during training and on some actual operations, I have asked both the team leader and team members who was responsible for a certain area and no one knew! This is another good reason teams that must train together. Get these problems fixed before going out on a real operation.

One security issue often overlooked during tactical movement is that of assigning someone to rear security. Many times I have observed teams moving to and from target sites, and the person responsible for the rear security rarely or never checks to make sure the team is not being followed. Often the team leader even fails to designate anyone as rear security. Team members assume that since they have moved through an area there is no one there and, hence, there is no reason to check the rear area. They are seriously mistaken. Just because you moved through an area and didn't see anyone doesn't always mean there wasn't someone there or that you weren't observed. You could have been observed from a distance and as a result someone might now be following you. Also, even if you are moving carefully as a small team you are going to leave some sign that you have traveled through the area. Unless you have the benefit of a strong wind and a heavy rain you will leave signs that even a moderately good tracker could follow. If you don't have someone who is very alert responsible for rear security, you are asking for trouble.

Even when some were designated as responsible for rear security, I have seen them fail to frequently check the rear area. I believe this is due to the fact that as the team is moving forward and is spread out, they are worried they will miss any hand and arm signals and may get left behind. Also, we aren't in the habit of frequently looking back as we move. It takes continuous effort to make ourselves keep checking to ensure that we aren't being followed. One of the best ways to work against a rural surveillance team is to track it and hit it from the rear since most of the team members are concentrating on where they are going

rather than where they have been. Those who are on the outer edges of the formation also need to frequently check behind to make sure no one is following the team from the rear.

ROUTE SELECTION

Good route selection can go a long way to ensuring successful tactical movement. Try to pick routes that are likely to avoid local residents, built-up areas, and possible hostile personnel. It is also important to try to travel over areas that avoid the natural lines of drift in the terrain. These lines of drift are where others are most likely to travel. Whenever possible, you should try to select alternate routes of travel in the event that you can't use your primary route. Any alternate routes selected need to be far enough away from each other that so that movement on both routes can't be detected from one location. Remember that your ultimate goal is to move to your target without being detected.

To select the best routes, study the area using the most up-to-date maps available. Although the terrain doesn't usually change much, other things often make a route unusable such as new roads or buildings. If the mission and time allow you to conduct a discreet aerial reconnaissance, you should do so. In most cases you will likely see some things you didn't know about the area, and this will give you a good opportunity to see the target and surrounding area from a different perspective. Also, it will allow you to see how thick the vegetation really is as opposed to how you think it may be or how the map reflects it.

When planning, you should try to select primary and alternate routes. As you select routes divide each route into legs. Periodically changing its direction of movement will help the team remain undetected.

For years the military has used the acronym OCOKA—observation, cover and concealment, obstacles, key terrain, and avenues of approach. This is a good term to remember and apply when you select a route or routes to follow into and out of a target area.

Use observation to choose routes that will likely allow your team to have good observation of the area and allow them to see others approaching. Avoid areas that expose you and your team to observation by others. *These areas may be dictated by the weather and the time of your activity.*

Use cover and concealment to select a route that provides you with adequate cover and concealment for your movement. Be careful not to select an area so thick with vegetation that you have to fight to get through it, resulting in making a lot of noise and leaving a trail a blind man could follow.

Avoid obstacles. Try to pick routes that will not impede your movement to the target or could compromise your team. Avoid deep, fast-moving rivers and streams, or areas with steep hills. Also avoid well-traveled roads and built-up areas.

Be aware of key terrain features in the area you are moving through that can be useful to you when navigating. Try to avoid these areas as they usually will have other people at or near them.

Try to avoid likely avenues of approach. If you are conducting a raid or a surveillance operation on someone that is trained or alert, he will be monitoring these likely approaches. This is particulary important if you have reason to believe the people you are working against may employ booby traps or security devices to detect intruders. As you plan your route and approach to the target area and the target itself, think about where you would expect someone to approach from and then try to select a different route.

TYPES OF TERRAIN

The type of terrain you are working in will dictate the routes you select. Just as moving in an area with lots of foliage in the summer is quite different than trying to move in the winter when the area provides little cover, so can various types of terrain change your plans.

Mountain areas offer advantages and disadvantages. Although they can provide cover and protection, they can also tire your team out and slow your progress. You may not be able to carry as much equipment as you would like, and there is a higher chance of injury when working in mountainous terrain. Also, you can hardly avoid cliffs and streams when traveling through this terrain. All these factors will have a direct impact on your team, especially if they are not familiar with working in this type of area. Dense foliage along mountain streams can also make travel extremely difficult.

Desert terrain often has little cover, so it can quickly limit your options for route selection. Even moving at night in an open area can make you vulnerable to detection, especially if there is moonlight.

Jungle areas offer unique challenges to those trying to move tactically. The ground is often soft and wet making it almost impossible to not leave a trail. The few roads and trails are heavily traveled by people, so it is important to avoid using them. Due to the high rainfall in a jungle area, the ground is slippery. Routes should follow ridgelines or low ground where movement is faster and less tiring.

Swamps have few features, which makes it necessary to travel using exact measurements from the compass and pace counts. If you have a detailed map of the swamp area you should try to take advantage of any high ground or island areas in the swamp. These can serve as rest or base camp areas. Be prepared to do lots of stream crossings, because swamps are usually full of streams.

Arctic terrain is often difficult to travel, plus there is little concealment. Whenever possible you should try to start as close to your objective as is tactically possible. The weather can be your best ally as well as your worst enemy; storms can mask your movement and at the same time threaten your operation.

COMMUNICATION AND CONTROL

I have often seen teams that have worked and trained together for a long time and yet don't have a practical, working set of hand and arm signals. Instead they depend solely on their radio gear to communicate. When I ask them about this they say it has almost always worked OK for them. When I ask them what they do when it *doesn't* work the answer is usually pretty weak. It is obvious that many teams are too dependent on radios for communication and are not comfortable or proficient in hand and arm signals. I'm not against radios, but I think they pose a risk to the team when used where the opposition may be using equipment to intercept transmissions. Teams can become too dependent on them, and too many electrical devices go down when used in a rural environment. Radios also encourage team members to BS with each other when they get bored and nothing is happening in the target area.

For my money, I would rather depend on visual hand and arm signals. You don't need more than 10 or 12 to be able to communicate and control the movement of the team. Hand and arm signals do not need to be complex; simple, well-rehearsed signals with simple meanings are enough. They also need to be tactical. Since rapid movement attracts the human eye, it is important that team members learn to give all signals in slow and deliberate ways rather than using sharp movements. At night or during times of limited visibility you should be closer together and whisper if necessary.

There are some who recommend using red filter lights, luminous tape, or infrared light to signal each other. I strongly disagree. If you are working against a target occupied by individuals who may have strong security you do not want to use any communication that could compromise you or members of the team.

RALLY POINTS

Rally points should be used whenever you conduct a tactical movement. These are locations in the target area where team members can meet and reorganize if they get separated or discovered. The points should be designated during mission planning even before the team is deployed on the ground in case something happens in the first few moments of deployment.

Normally the team leader selects new rally points while moving to the target area, as well as when leaving the area. The points should be easy to recognize, offer cover and concealment, be defensible for at least a short time, and be away from areas people are likely to travel. As a team moves through an area the team leader may recognize a location along the route that makes a good rally point; he can alert the team that this will be the rally area.

If the situation is such that the last rally point can't be used, the team should use the rally point previously designated. It is a good idea to set a time limit to how long a team will wait at a rally point before it moves on. Obviously the use of rally points must be integrated into your training routine.

DANGER AREAS

Anytime you conduct a tactical movement to a target for rural surveillance you will likely encounter danger areas—places that could expose the team to others in the area or make the team vulnerable to detection. Examples of such areas are roads, open fields, trails, or streams. Ideally, the team should avoid these areas or skirt around them. This isn't always possible, as in the case of a road or wide stream. When it is necessary to cross a danger area, every effort should be made to do so at a point where the team is least visible, such as at a curve in a road. If there is a location where foliage comes right up to the danger area and allows more cover for the team, use it.

There are a number of different methods for crossing danger areas and the one you decide to use is up to you. The important thing is to practice several ways and then select the one that works best for your team. It is something you need to practice as a team to become proficient.

Once your point man sees and signals that there is a danger area ahead, the first thing you need to do is to designate near-side and far-side rally points. These are where team

Clear, easily understandable hand signals are valuable additions to your communications procedures. Practice them regularly.

members can meet if the team is attacked or has to disperse immediately before, after, or during the time they are crossing the danger area. I recommend that you develop a standard team procedure for handling this type of situation and then practice it together. For example, you may decide to regroup 200 meters from the point where you attempted to cross the danger area on the side you approached from. Practice this frequently; it's too late to try and work it out once you are on an operation. Also determine what actions you will follow if the team gets split up during the crossing. If you have part of the team on one side and part on the other, where should they try to link up?

The size of your rural surveillance team will likely dictate the method you will use to cross a danger area. If your group is small—four to six strong—I recommend the following: Have your point man and one other cross over together and check to ensure that the other side is safe. After they signal that all is secure, you can come across in groups of two or three until the entire team is safely across. Once on the other side, take a moment to see if you were followed and to make sure everyone is together. This is also a good time to check to make sure no one is missing any equipment. I have seen teams run across small danger areas and drop pieces of equipment in the middle of a well-traveled dirt road. This is not a good thing! Walk quickly, but don't run across a danger area.

Remember, one of the biggest threats to a rural surveillance operation is being detected by personnel in the area. This is most likely to happen in or around danger areas. It is important that your team rehearses how it will work together to negotiate these potential threats. Practice this often.

BASE CAMPS

If you are going to spend more than a few hours on a target you need to establish some sort of base camp. Choosing a location for a base camp is different than selecting a site to rest overnight. The time to start selecting a base camp is during the mission-planning phase of the operation. Its exact location may change once you get into the area, but you should beginning planning where you want to set it up as soon as possible.

The most critical consideration in site selection is security. Be sure to recon the site and the surrounding area before you occupy it. Once occupied, make sure that those on security remain alert at all times. Choose an area where it is unlikely for others to be or have a reason to go. Find a remote or out-of-the-way spot that is difficult for people to get to and where the approach of an intruder is easily detected. Your base camp should have good concealment with vegetation that also protects you from observation from above. Select a place far from human habitation, if possible, and near a good source of water. Try to avoid trails, roads, and lines of drift—those areas such as ridgelines where it's easier, and therefore more common, to travel. It is also a good idea to have an alternate site picked out just in case your camp is compromised or the operation continues longer and you need to find another site.

Maintaining a high level of alertness for a long period can be difficult for some. I have seen base camps that started to look like a Boy Scout campground after a couple of days; team members started getting comfortable and feeling that when they were in the base camp they were secure. Nothing could be further from the truth. In fact, a team is actually more vulnerable when in base camp than when they are on the target. This is because when on the target they are being as cautious as possible; they are alert to the threat and are trying hard to remain undetected. But when team members return to camp, they are tired and all they want to do is get something to eat and go to sleep. They relax, and that's when they are vulnerable.

Don't let this happen on your operation. Post security and frequently check to make sure they are alert. Have a plan for what you will do if the base camp is discovered. Check to ensure that all keep their weapons and equipment put up when not in use so that in the event they are discovered, the team can leave the area immediately. Practice maintaining a secure base camp at all times.

- Check the area around your base camp for signs of other people/activity.
- Have one point of entry into and out of the camp, but establish alternate escape routes for emergencies.
- Restrict movement both in and outside the camp.
- Allow fires only when absolutely necessary, and never at night unless it's an emergency.
- The best time for a fire is around noon when the air is thin and smoke dissipates quickly. Build the fire low and conceal it from sight as much as possible.
- Use dry, hard, deadwood because it gives off the least amount of smoke.
- Strictly enforce camouflage for the camp and team members.
- Enforce noise and light discipline.
- Keep all gear packed and be ready to leave at a moment's notice.
- Set up a location for sanitation and personal hygiene outside the base camp.
- Try to have at least two team members in the camp at all times.
- Keep all garbage stored and covered.
- When leaving, make sure nothing is left behind.

When the operation is completed, you must ensure that the base camp and all observation and hide sites are sanitized. As you begin your tactical movement out of the area, follow the same tactical movement techniques you used when you entered.

TRAINING

Training and preparation are the keys to conducting a successful tactical movement against a real target. In my experience, even the best teams run into problems they had not thought of in training but were able to overcome

them because they had worked together and knew what to do as a team. Don't depend on luck! You are putting the operation, the team, and yourself at risk if you don't prepare and train to move tactically in a high-threat environment. And don't forget, they're *all* high-threat environments. The following tips are provided to assist you in moving securely on a rural surveillance operation.

TIPS FOR TACTICAL MOVEMENT

The following tips can improve your tactical movement both individually and as a team. These are points I recommend that have worked for me and have proven to help ensure success. I hope they are helpful to you and your team.

- Never move in a straight line, but rather in a general direction.
- Don't set a predictable pattern during movement.
- Whenever possible, use prominent terrain features to aid your navigation.
- Establish and maintain a buddy system at all times. Adjust the buddy system as the mission or events dictate.
- Designate who will take care of each man and his equipment if he is injured or wounded.
- Never smoke while on a rural surveillance mission; the odor will give you and your team away.
- The team leader should remind each man of the primary and alternate rally points before darkness. The team must have primary and alternate rally points at all times throughout the mission.
- Never be afraid to move at night. Darkness is one of your best aids.
- Keep foods and liquids in airtight, resealable containers. Have a spare container for foods.
- Never prepare food or drink with strong odors while on a mission.
- Prior to darkness, memorize the location of prominent terrain features, large trees, etc., and the azimuth to them.

- Make sure you have a compass that works well at night and practice using it.
- Once you decide on a base camp or a site to rest overnight, all personnel should keep their equipment on and be alert until the perimeter has been checked out to a distance of 30 to 40 meters in 360 degrees.
- No packs should be removed until dark has fallen.
- Use indigenous sounds and weather to help conceal your movement.
- Avoid terrain that would allow your team to get trapped or pinned down.
- Fishhook just prior to setting up for the night. To accomplish this, travel some distance past the area where you plan to set up your camp, then turn back parallel to the trail you just traveled, coming back to the spot you chose. This will allow you to see if you are being followed.
- When stopping for more than just a few minutes, check around your position.
- Never leave a position without ensuring you didn't leave something behind.
- During an overnight stop, each man should be close enough to touch the man on either side without changing his position.
- Never get spooked into moving.
- If a team member snores, make him sleep with a protective mask on.
- Avoid using trails at all costs.
- Be careful crossing streams; try not to muddy the water or knock debris into the water.
- When being picked up, maintain 360-degree security at all times. Assume you are going to be attacked. Most teams let their guard down at this time. Don't do it!
- Objectively critique all missions and training missions upon completion. Don't hold back. Encourage team members to be honest and direct.
- Never cook or build heating fires unless there is an emergency.
- Each team member must continually observe the man in front and the man behind and watch for other team members' hand and arm signals.

- Watch for heat injuries, hypothermia, and immersion foot. These are all mission stoppers.
- Never do the obvious.
- Have several pen lights with red filters per team.
- Every chance you get, check all your equipment. Ensure that team members do the same.
- Treat all trails, streams, and open areas as danger areas.
- Always carry your maps, notes, etc., in a waterproof container.
- Don't mark on your map and don't allow team members to mark on theirs.
- Make sure that everything you carry is silent when opened.
- Have a good ground pad and a good sleeping cover.
- Rehearse loading and unloading vehicles frequently. Have it down!
- During dry season, do not urinate on rocks or leaves. Urinate in a hole or small crevice.
- When getting water, have one man collect the canteens, move to the water, and fill them. Have someone go with him to provide security.
- Memorize the trees and bushes around you prior to darkness. Things look different in the dark.
- Always use the water in your rucksack first.
- Personnel should not eat at the same time. While one eats, the other is security.
- Try never to break branches of trees or bushes.
- Never use small trees to steady yourself or pull yourself up a hill.
- Make yourself slow down when operating in a rural environment.
- Don't fire your weapon at night unless absolutely necessary.
- Don't worry about retrieving the first few magazines when in contact.
- Whenever possible, use a reference point when taking pictures.
- Test-fire all weapons before going on an operation.

- Check and test all equipment before leaving on an operation.
- Oil the selector switch on weapons daily and quietly work them back and forth. Carry your weapon with the selector switch on safe.
- Quietly change the cartridge in the chamber of your weapon each time prior to going on watch.
- Travel light, carrying only the equipment needed for the mission and the weather.
- Take everything you will need yourself. Do not try to use the good neighbor policy.
- Ensure that everything taken on an operation is sterile and nonattributable. For example, if you are with a sheriff's department, don't allow anything to be labeled or identifiable as belonging to that (or any) department. Don't even allow names on clothes or equipment that could be traced back to the unit or the individual.
- Always carry a good field knife with you. It should be nonreflective.
- A pair of lightweight gloves should be worn when in the field to protect your hands and to aid in camouflage. It's a good idea to have a second pair. They must provide protection but allow for the manipulation of all equipment.
- Take more than one cleaning kit per team for all weapons.
- Use dark, nonreflective tape to keep equipment from making noise.
- Once equipment is inspected and packed for an operation, store it in a secure area.
- Pack extra socks plus foot powder. Be careful using the powder in the field.
- Consider alternate/multiple uses for everything you pack.
- Ensure that the team has materials that can double to make a stretcher.
- Keep radio traffic to a minimum and ensure that those communicating with your team understand the importance of this.
- Before talking on the radio, know what you are going to say.

- Waterproof all your communications gear.
- Check all your communications gear before leaving the launch site to ensure that it's functioning.
- Make sure you have complete medical kits for each team member as well as for the team.
- Double-check that all team members have the gear your SOP requires.
- All survival gear should be secured in pockets, not rucksacks. Noiseproof it.
- Know the contents of your first-aid kits as well as all equipment kits you take.
- Have plenty of insect repellant and apply it to dry clothing prior to deploying.
- Be sure to bring cough suppressant medicine for all team members.
- Foot powder or petroleum jelly rubbed into the feet will help prevent blisters as well as immersion foot during wet weather.
- Ensure that all team members have several pairs of padded socks and change them frequently. They should never change at the same time or do both feet at the same time.
- Emphasize and practice teamwork in all things that you and your team attempt.
- Ensure team and individual proficiencies in all areas.
- Maintain yourself and your team at a high degree of physical fitness.
- Train as a team frequently and stress realism in training at all times.
- Don't be afraid to take or give advice and suggestions. Encourage this!
- Always have at least one alternate plan.
- Stay alert at all times.
- Never lose your temper.
- Guard against being overly confident.
- Don't be too regimented. Be prepared to adjust to a changing situation.
- If you show confidence, your team will have confidence.
- Know that fear is a natural instinct.
- Check everything at least twice.
- Train and rehearse for every situation you can imagine to prevent possible team and individual deficiencies before they occur in the field. Make sure that each

team member knows his duties and the duties of every other team member in any given situation.

- Ensure that all team members and equipment are sterile before departure on an operation.
- Take your time to analyze and evaluate your plans and procedures.
- During an operation, take time to review what has occurred and what your plans are.
- Work at staying focused on the operation but do not lose sight of the big picture.
- Avoid unnecessary risks.
- Take your time; do not allow your team or yourself to become too tired. Remember that tired men become careless and make mistakes.
- Plan ahead. Know what you will do tonight and tomorrow, but stay flexible.
- Wear loose-fitting clothing. Tight clothes restrict movement and will rip.
- The team leader must check everything. Help him do that.
- The team leader should be the first man on the ground during insertion and the last to load up when leaving the operational area.
- Develop a pre- and a postmission checklist to ensure that you don't forget anything. Use this list each time you go out for training or on an operation.
- Never assume your weapon is clean enough to function. Always clean your weapon before moving to the surveillance target.
- Make sure all snaps and buckles are camouflaged.
- Test the straps on all your equipment. Each man should carry several yards of parachute cord to tie things and make repairs with.
- Use a sturdy waterproof bag inside your rucksack to protect its contents from rain or during a stream crossing. Heavy, black plastic trash bags are good for this purpose.
- Isolate items in your rucksack that might leak. Put them in waterproof bags in case they rupture.

- If you must cough, do it in your hat to cover the sound.
- Do not throw away anything while on an operation or exercise. Pack out everything you take into the area.
- All team members should take notes while on an operation and compare them nightly. Each man should keep a list of tips and lessons learned and add to them after each operation. This will make a tremendous difference to the team over time.
- Avoid overconfidence—it leads to carelessness. Just because you think you haven't been discovered doesn't mean you can't be.
- Correct all team and individual errors as they occur. Correct them in a professional manner.
- If you stop for a rest, do not take your gear off or lay your weapon down.
- The team leader must ensure that each member gets plenty of water and enough to eat.
- It is a good idea to have all members take a multi-vitamin each day they are out in the field.
- If team members require glasses or contacts, have them bring two sets. Require them to take glasses, because contacts are difficult to work with in the field.
- During movement it is a good idea to wear a set of clear goggles to protect the eyes, especially when moving at night through brush.
- Review what you have done in the preceding several hours and days and make sure you aren't setting predictable patterns to your activities.
- Move only as fast as the heaviest loaded man can move.
- No individual or team can practice or train too much.

Remember that attitude is everything! There is nothing you and your team can't do with the right attitude!

Chapter Seven:
Cover, Concealment,
and Camouflage

When people discuss cover, concealment, and camouflage they often use the terms interchangeably. This is not accurate. In this chapter I want to focus primarily on the subject of camouflage. If you are going to conduct any type of rural operation that requires you to remain undetected you must have a clear understanding of what each of these terms means and how they will aid you during a rural operation. Likewise, if you are planning to conduct a raid in a rural environment, you must master these capabilities. Not doing so will put you and your teammates at great risk.

COVER

Cover is any structure or solid object, natural or man-made, that can afford protection from direct fire or from fragmentation. It can be a large tree, a boulder, a vehicle, or a ditch. I have heard people say that they "took cover" behind a bush when the firing started. They would have been dead wrong if the bullets had come their way. What, in fact they were doing was getting a little concealment—not taking cover. Your definition of cover should be determined by the penetrating capabilities of the weapons that could be used or are being used against you. Good cover is distinguished by form, thickness, and density. Many people put themselves in a very dangerous situation by not having a healthy appreciation for the penetrating power of an enemy's weapons. They make the mistake of believing that if they can't be seen they can't be shot.

One of the first things I do, whenever possible, is select an observation site that offers or is near good cover. There have been times when this simply was not possible, but it is one of the things you should consider. Should you suddenly find yourself in a tactical situation, select cover that gives you the flexibility to move if you have to. A good cover position is one that does not leave you so confined that you can't move to another position if you have to. If you have to move some distance from one covered position to another, try to use any other available cover to do so.

When the need to take cover arises, it is important for you to be able to keep a good eye on the suspect and his position. If you can't, there is the possibility he may leave his position undetected and escape or, worse, move to a position where he has a clear shot at you. Be sure to pick cover that affords you the opportunity to observe, return fire, advance, or retreat as needed. Try to envision—from the suspect's perspective—how the cover may protect you. What you may think is adequate cover may not be so from his position. This is a particularly important point for cover as well as concealment and camouflage. Remember to evaluate your position from the likely perspective of those you put under surveillance.

CONCEALMENT

Concealment is anything already in the area that protects you from being observed. Concealment alone won't keep you from being shot but it can keep you from being shot at, since it's much more difficult for someone to shoot what he can't see. Good concealment should keep someone from even knowing you are there.

There are any number of things that can aid in concealment; darkness is one of the best. Anytime you can use darkness you should do so. Shadows are another aid to concealment. Even during daylight hours shadows from buildings, trees, and other objects can help. Rain and the wind are very beneficial to concealment because they limit visibility as well as noise. But keep in mind that wind may give you away depending on its direction. Strong odors from insect repellant or other sources may be enough to alert someone to your presence.

Good concealment requires you to think about it and practice it constantly. It takes real discipline to remain concealed for any length of time. The three keys to concealment are noise, light, and movement discipline. You must control these aspects of your activities or else you and your team will eventually be compromised.

Noise Discipline

Noise discipline means taking action to silence or reduce sounds from your movement and location. It begins before you leave and requires all team members to develop a mind-set against making any unnecessary noise while in an operational area. This mind-set must be instilled in every team member during training exercises before an actual operation. Noise discipline should be considered as each member is packing his equipment for the operation—care should be taken to make sure items in packs and pockets don't rattle or make noise while moving. Filling canteens so they don't make sloshing noises is a good example of the care that should be taken to prevent noise in the field. Using oil or graphite to prevent metal parts from creating unnecessary noise is another example.

Using noises around you while conducting an operation is a type of noise discipline. If a loud jet plane is passing overhead, it may afford an opportunity to move using its noise to mask your activity. I was once on a target between the house under observation and a busy road and was able to use the noise of the traffic to mask our movement. However, on the other side of the house it was unusually quiet. You have to be careful about depending on other sounds to aid in noise discipline.

Light Discipline

Light discipline involves controlling the use of lights as well as minimizing or eliminating any reflections. Team members should inspect each other's gear to ensure that no one is carrying anything that might reflect or emit light that can't be controlled. Even the smallest amount of light can be observed for a long distance at night. Luminous sights on weapons can also be seen from a distance if not properly covered. From habit many officers are conditioned to rely on flashlights at night or when visibility is limited. In most environments this can be a great aid, but in a rural operation it can be deadly. If you must use a light to look at a map, use one with a red or blue filter and get on the ground and under a poncho before turning it on. Shine and reflections may also violate light discipline. To prevent this, everyone must maintain his camouflage at all times. As I will discuss later, the hand or face that is not properly camouflaged can quickly give away a location; the reflection from a shiny piece of equipment will catch the human eye and reveal your location. Remember, very little in nature shines, reflects, or emits light, so take measures to ensure that you and your team do not stand out or draw attention to yourselves.

Movement Discipline

Movement discipline involves a number of techniques designed to ensure that your position is not discovered. When it is necessary to move, you should stay as low as possible and try to select routes that can shield you from observation. A key to movement discipline is to move slowly. It may be difficult but just as in tracking you must slow your mind down; it is better to move slowly and safely than to try to hurry and risk being spotted. Rapid movements attract the human eye much more than slow, deliberate movements, and you should always assume that the area you are moving through is under observation by others. Discipline yourself and your team to stop, look, and listen often. Make an effort not to cause the overhead movement of trees, bushes, or tall grass by rubbing against them. As stated before, move during vehicle or aircraft noise, wind, or any other noise that might distract or conceal your movement.

CAMOUFLAGE

The U.S. Army calls camouflage one of the basic weapons of war. When you think about that it makes a lot of sense. In a rural operation, just as in war, camouflage can make the difference between success and failure. It may even mean the difference between life and death. The dictionary defines camouflage as "disguising to conceal, as by the use of paint, nets, leaves, etc. in patterns merging with the background." During a rural surveillance operation you must be camouflage-conscious from the time you begin planning to the time you leave the area. At no time can you let your guard down. Camouflage is an integral part of your security; it is like a security blanket and you must keep it with you the entire time you are on an operation.

There are two basic types of camouflage that you can use to conceal yourself and your equipment during a rural surveillance operation. These are *natural* camouflage and *artificial* camouflage.

Natural camouflage consists of vegetation and materials that are natural to the area you are operating in. A good rural surveillance team should always augment its appearance whenever practical by making use of natural camouflage, but this does not necessarily mean you should cover yourself with branches from bushes and trees in the area. I was recently training a group, and one individual covered

himself with limbs and leaves so much that he actually drew attention to himself when he moved. He looked like a moving plant arrangement. I applaud his effort, but you can overdo it. The goal is to blend in.

If you are in a hot climate, leaves and branches you use to cover yourself will quickly wilt. When this happens, you have to gather more foliage to cover yourself with. This can present you with other problems, since moving out of the area to get additional foliage and disposing of the wilted vegetation could give you away.

It is almost always better to have a good set of camouflage clothing that blends in well with the natural foliage you are in rather than trying to look exactly like one of the bushes in the area. Using only a small amount of the natural foliage to augment your camouflage and break up your pattern is usually the best thing. Dirt or mud on the skin and clothing also makes an excellent natural camouflage.

Artificial camouflage is any material or outfit produced for the purpose of coloring or covering something to conceal it. Even darkened mosquito netting can be an excellent artificial camouflage. There are countless types of artificial camouflage material on the commercial market; some of it is good and some is lousy. If you are planning to purchase any I recommend that you first know how and where you want to employ it. Visit the area and get a good idea in your mind of what the natural vegetation looks like before you purchase any artificial camouflage. Don't forget that you must also camouflage your pack and other equipment as well as the clothes you will wear. Many times, people go to the field wearing excellent camouflage clothing under equipment that stands out in contrast to the area they are in.

Camouflage sticks and face paints are another type of artificial camouflage. When used properly, these can greatly benefit an individual trying to blend into the surroundings. But it is important to remember that you are not going to a fashion show— don't try to look like a poster boy for military

Blending in is the key to concealment. These team members are wearing ghillie suits that closely mimic the low brush at the edge of a clearing.

recruiting. Simply darkening the hands, neck, face, and any other exposed skin should be sufficient to help you to blend with the area.

The techniques of camouflage involve a combination of hiding and blending. Hiding is completely concealing the body from observation. You can accomplish this by lying in a hole, ditch, or wooded area and covering yourself with leaves and dirt. You can also accomplish this by using thick vegetation in the area and sitting in the middle of it. This is more limiting but can be used effectively in certain circumstances that call for extreme measures. I have sat in very thick bushes for hours in urban settings where people were constantly walking by not more than a few feet away. This, of course, can only be done with very large, thick vegetation but it is possible. Depending on the circumstances, you may want to ensure that the vegetation provides cover completely around you. Also make sure that your feet can be hidden and that the cover will support your weight. It is critical that you not put yourself in a situation where you could be trapped and captured as a result of having no avenue of escape.

Blending is the technique used more often when employing camouflage. Since it is not always possible to camouflage yourself to the point that you are indistinguishable from your surroundings, blending is the next best option. When blending, your goal should be to camouflage yourself so that you cannot be recognized by the naked eye or by someone using optics from a distance, and who is looking directly at you. This is one point I always try to make to those I train. Keep in mind that those who may be looking in your direction may not know you are there and *won't* know you are there unless you give them a reason to. Blend into your surroundings and you will be amazed how people will look directly at you and not see you.

There are some fundamentals to camouflage, and paying close attention to them is the mark of a good surveillance operator. Much of it is common sense and being observant of your surroundings.

- Use only as much camouflage material (natural or artificial) as is needed. Too much camouflage can make you and your hide site stand out almost as much as not having enough.
- Study the terrain and vegetation around you and arrange brush, leaves, limbs, and other such materials in a way that conforms to the surroundings.
- If using natural material, gather it from a large area. If you strip it from one area it will attract attention, especially from anyone who is familiar with the area.
- Try not to displace the soil when developing a hide site. Disturbed soil or piles of fresh dirt indicate an area has been occupied. You want to leave a site as you found it.
- Remember that in many locations the vegetation changes with the seasons, so what served as camouflage at one time may not be good during another time of the year.
- Using good man-made camouflage materials and concealment techniques will usually allow you occupy a hide site without having to disturb the natural vegetation.

Part of the trick to learning how to effectively camouflage yourself and your team is by having an aggressive policy concerning camouflage. One way you do this is by conducting camouflage exercises in which the team moves through an area that is being observed by other team members. When I train teams in rural surveillance operations one of the exercises we use is to divide teams up to work against each other. In addition to creating some competitive spirit, it forces each student to work on his individual camouflage. One group is allowed to move into an area and select a site from which it can observe. The other group is required to move through the area and try to spot the other team before being spotted. At the completion of each exercise both sides brief the other as to who saw what and why it drew their attention. They are given some time to fix what gave them away and are

 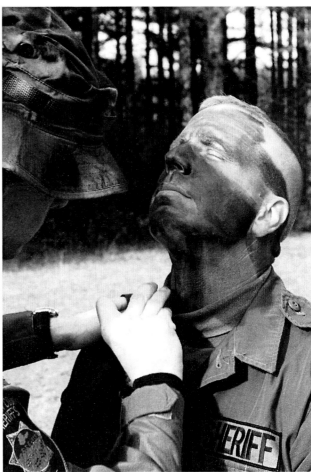

Whether you use fabric or paint, your face must be concealed. Any exposed skin will be highly visible and must be treated.

then allowed to go at each other again. It is a good idea to mix the teams up frequently to keep the exercises interesting and challenging. By being spotted and told what it was that gave them away they can adjust and improve their camouflage to make it better. This allows teams to fix any camouflage deficiencies in a non-threatening environment. It also conditions team members to check each other's camouflage. Having a team become compromised, even in a training exercise, can be a great motivator for all team members to take their individual camouflage seriously.

Camouflage will vary depending on the geographical areas you may be required to work in. Weather will also make it unrealistic to use the same camouflage kit all the time. From my experience, if there is any one camouflage material that comes closest to

being the best overall pattern, it would be a gray and black woodland pattern. Even that is not going to be ideal for some areas or weather conditions. The following are suggestions for camouflage that will likely work in various areas based upon conditions such as weather, season, and vegetation.

Many desert and some coastal areas are sandy and have very little vegetation. Textured camouflage patterns are only going to make you stand out. A suit that blends with the colors of the area and breaks up the human form is needed in this environment. A blend of tan and brown colors is going to be most effective but the colors should not be so strong or bright that they draw attention to themselves. Ideally, a bulky smock-type uniform with a hood made of light colors will work well in this type of environment.

In areas with heavy snow, such as open fields, you can use a full white camouflage suit with gray shading. This could serve you well if you are conducting a surveillance that is not going to last several days. If you find yourself in an area where there is a large snow accumulation with much of the surrounding brush and limbs also covered, the full white suit with gray shading may also serve as a good camouflage. In wooded areas where the snow is all on the ground, white trousers with a green and brown or a green and gray top may be your best bet for good camouflage. For these snow-covered areas it is suggested that you employ a white and gray hood or veil. It is very important that your pack, weapon, and any other equipment you are carrying also be camouflaged mostly white. Remember that during the night in regions where there is a lot of snow on the ground, a clear sky can make it seem almost like day. Don't make the mistake of thinking you have the cover of darkness.

In a jungle environment you may use a combination of foliage, camouflage material, and camouflage paint to give yourself a pattern that blends in with the surroundings. Since jungle environments are hot and humid, you are going to be sweating a lot even if you remain still most of the time, so any camouflage paint you apply to your skin will likely be sweated away more quickly. You should wear camouflage clothing that is light and loose fitting, since a heavy set of clothing or a thick ghillie suit will cause you to lose too much body fluid. One major advantage in a jungle environment is that there is usually plenty of vegetation to work with.

GHILLIE SUITS

Many people today believe that to be fully camouflaged in the woods you need a ghillie suit, which originated in Scotland where game wardens wore them to conceal themselves from poachers. Today hunters and military personnel, especially snipers, use ghillie suits. There are a number of manufactured suits; some are very good, though most are very expensive. I know several law enforcement officers who have taken the initiative to make their own and do so after carefully observing the areas they are likely to operate in.

Although ghillie suits are great camouflage tools, especially when you are in a stationary position, they are not always the best for rural surveillance operations. If you are going to

When camouflage is used correctly, an entire team can blend into an area undetected.

A ghillie suit that is well matched to the terrain and vegetation can make you nearly invisible.

move any distance you will not want to do it in a ghillie suit. Most are very heavy and can get hot, even when you are lying still. Also, they can snag on limbs and branches while you are trying to move quietly. But they can be mission savers when you're on an extended surveillance operation and need to remain closely on your target for long periods.

If you elect to make your own suit, you can do so fairly cheaply. One method is to start with military field clothes or a loose-fitting one-piece aviator uniform. Turn the garment inside out so the pockets are on the inside next to your body. Make sure all buttons, zippers, belt loops, and pocket flaps are sewn on securely. You may even want to double-stitch anything that could possibly get torn off. You should also pad or add extra layers of the same type of material to the knee, thigh, elbow, butt, and stomach areas. This will protect against wear and tear when lying or crawling. Some people use canvas to protect these areas since it will take more abuse and last longer. It is a good idea to use heavy nylon thread to sew these extra layers to the garment.

Next, select the netting or material you will sew to the uniform. This should blend in with your environment. (Keep in mind that what may work during one season may give you away during another part of the year.) This material should be sewn on securely and vary in length depending on what part of the suit you sew it to. Make sure that the material you sew to the back of the suit is long enough to cover the sides when you are lying in a prone position. There should also be several overlapping layers of material strips to aid the camouflage effect.

Incorporate some type of hood or attached head cover as part of the suit to conceal and protect the head and neck; make it capable of being thrown back if necessary. This headpiece should have the same type of material sewn to it as the rest of the suit. Cut-up pieces of canvas or old cloth make excellent garnish materials. This headpiece should also have a veil attached (mosquito netting works well) that you can pull over your face and see through; this will allow you to be covered and still observe the target. It should be long enough to cover your face as well as your binoculars or any other optic device you

This team member's ghillie suit has rough burlap strips from head to toe, allowing him to blend in easily with the pale tan grass shoots.

Homemade ghillie suits are often the best kind, because they can be adapted to each new environment.

use. It also will help protect you from insects, which could cause you to make unnecessary movements that could give away your position. When using a ghillie suit remember that it is only a foundation for your camouflage. Never depend solely on the suit to hide you. Utilize the surrounding vegetation and terrain to help blend in with your surroundings.

MASTERING CAMOUFLAGE

Like so many other rural surveillance skills, the best way to learn and master camouflage skills is by trial and error. The best that can be expected from this text is to provide you with a starting point. Apply what is described here and learn what does and doesn't work for you.

When preparing for and using camouflage you must remember that it is designed to address the following aspects.

Shape must be disguised. You must break up the shape of the body, particularly the head.

Wearing certain types of hats will help, but they need to have their shape broken up as well. Use small amounts of natural brush or camouflage material to break up your human shape and the shape of weapons and equipment.

Shadows of a human form in a natural environment will draw attention. A shadow may be seen even when the body casting it is concealed. Depending on the angle of the light to the body, the shadow may be much larger than the actual body. Also, the movement of the shadow draws attention just as the movement of the body would.

Silhouettes can give you away and under certain conditions can be seen great distances. Silhouettes are caused by being backlit or from a uniform contrasting sharply with its background. Allowing silhouettes to be seen on the horizon is one of the biggest mistakes made in the field. This is why you should move below ridgelines rather than on open ridgelines when traveling.

If you master the art of camouflage, you may never be seen. There's a surveillance-team member dead center in this photograph, but he's nearly invisible.

Shine is one of the biggest giveaways in a rural setting. Shine draws attention to itself more easily than anything else. Even a small amount of shine can be seen from a great distance. Every team member must eliminate sources of shine on his person and equipment.

Surfaces can draw attention to you if they are not broken up. A solid surface must be broken to blend in with the surrounding environment. Material must be the type that absorbs light rather than reflecting it. To blend in, be sure to break up the pattern from surfaces of your clothing and equipment.

Spacing is important for camouflage purposes just as it is important for security reasons. Keep team members from bunching up whenever possible. It is easier to see a large group moving together than individuals. It is also important to avoid regularity. This is not natural in a rural area and will also draw attention.

Smell and strong odors can compromise even the most well concealed and camouflaged team. Tobacco, cologne, shaving cream, insect repellant, foods, and weapons lubricants are just some of the items that can give you away. Keep in mind the direction of the wind in relation to you and the target. Make sure you don't take items with you that have a smell strong enough to alert others that you are in the area.

When practicing camouflage, remember that the real goal is to manage the perception of those you wish to hide from. When people look at objects they normally see things individually only if those items stand out individually. If a person looks at a tree in the middle of a field he sees the tree, but if he looks at a large group of trees he sees a forest. If you look at a crowd of people, you notice some because they stand out, but many others don't even draw your attention. That is the way you want to be with your camouflage.

You want to blend in and appear to be just another part of the landscape. When a person looks out into the woods his brain is analyzing visual information, looking for an item that draws his attention. As humans we tend to notice something that is a separate object. When we do notice a well-camouflaged person in the woods we realize how he stands out and wonder how we didn't see him in the first place. Once you know someone is there your mind begins to see that person and the surrounding area differently. This is the key to why blending in is so important and why these principles are so critical. We don't want our targets looking out and seeing individual items, we want them only to see the "forest."

Remember that camouflage is one of your best weapons as well as one of your best defenses. If you don't take it seriously and adopt a 100 percent camouflage policy, you will fail on a rural surveillance operation. Your success depends on your ability to remain concealed. Camouflage is like so many other points discussed in this book; if you don't practice it often you will not master it. If you don't become a master of camouflage you can't conduct a long-term rural surveillance mission.

Chapter Eight:
Tracking and Countertracking

Any rural surveillance team must employ tracking and countertracking techniques to ensure success. Team members should know what to look for and be able to recognize whether someone has recently passed through an area. They also need to grasp the basic principles of tracking in order to understand how they may be leaving signs of their activities and location. An awareness of tracking will give you a stronger appreciation for rear security and how important it is to the survival of an operation.

It is next to impossible to move through an area and not leave some sign that you were there. Even if you and your team leave only small signs, an experienced tracker can usually detect them. Also remember that you may be operating in an area very well known to the people you are working against and that they could notice signs indicating someone had been or is in the area. This doesn't mean you can't operate in the area, it just means you must be aware of signs you are leaving and how to minimize them. If you understand tracking techniques, there are deception drills you can employ that may confuse someone tracking you.

This chapter is not intended to make you an expert tracker or even a good tracker. That isn't possible, no matter how much detail is written about the subject. Tracking is another one of those skills that involves understanding the principles and then practicing them in the field. It can be difficult and frustrating, but the payoff can be great whether it is in the form of a successful rural surveillance operation,

tracking an escaped prisoner, or locating a lost child. Tracking has so many positive applications that I find it surprising that every sheriff's office in the country doesn't have several experienced, well-trained trackers in their departments.

Tracking is the ability to follow people or animals by the signs they leave. Everyone leaves some kind of sign as he moves through an area. When a team carrying weapons and equipment goes through an area with lots of vegetation or difficult terrain, it can't help leaving numerous signs; the larger the group, the more signs it will leave. And even small signs can be detected and followed by an experienced tracker. A good tracker can determine how many people he is following, how they are equipped, their sizes, their conditioning, and how well trained they are. He can often determine if those he is following are attempting to use countertracking techniques. For a rural surveillance team, it is important to know that if you have an experienced tracker following you, it is extremely difficult to get him off your trail. The only options you may have could be to discontinue the operation or capture the tracker.

TRACKING SKILLS

Trackers are made, not born, and someone must first have the desire and aptitude to become a good tracker; not everyone on your team will have what it takes. Those unique individuals who become good trackers must have great powers of observation and enormous patience. This is not to say that they always move slowly, but they do know when to slow down and really observe the signs in front of them.

When we discuss tracking with students during rural surveillance training, one of the first things we tell them is that they must slow their minds down. In other words, they must take a few minutes to see what is there in front of them and understand what it means. Too many people who try to track someone want to see a sign right away and move on as quickly as possible to the next easily recognizable track or sign. In so doing, they miss other tracks that may reveal more information about those they are tracking. It is important to move as quickly as is feasible when tracking and close the gap between yourself and your quarry, but not at the expense of missing other signs and contaminating the trail. A good tracker knows when to be patient.

A good tracker must have keen eyesight. He must know what he is looking for and be able to recognize it when he sees it. Those with limited vision usually don't make very good trackers, and those with vision problems are practically useless during night tracking operations. A tracker should not be colorblind. If you are tracking someone who is injured or wounded, color blindness may prevent you from seeing blood left along the trail.

Trackers should be in excellent physical condition. Tracking someone over a distance requires the tracker, as well as other members of the tracking team such as security, to be in top-notch condition. If there has been a period of time that allowed your quarry to gain a good distance between you and them, you have to keep moving to close that lead while the quarry may be resting. When the quarry stops to rest, you will have to keep going without rest and you will have to move faster if you are to catch up. This takes a great deal of stamina, and if you aren't in exceptional physical condition, a determined adversary may escape.

The best trackers I have seen are those who are comfortable in the woods and know how to employ stealth. They know the fundamentals of concealment and camouflage and they employ them at all times. Remember that your tracking team is only as good as the weakest member of the team. If the entire team doesn't move with stealth, you will likely be detected. If you don't employ and enforce a 100 percent camouflage policy, the team will probably be spotted. Keep this in mind as you move along on a trail.

Tracking Signs

Signs are visible marks left by a person passing through an area. There are ground signs, high signs, temporary signs, and permanent signs.

Ground signs are those signs or tracks that are left on the ground or no higher than the knee. Often you will find these where someone stepped over a fallen tree or where he brushed against the side of a tree and scraped away some of the bark.

High signs, or top signs, are those signs that are above the knee. These can be caused by a number of things, such as someone's weapon or pack breaking a limb or a tree limb being twisted or broken by someone grabbing it to pull himself up a hill. Often, trackers will become so focused on looking at the ground for tracks and signs that they fail to notice an obvious high sign that is right in front of them.

Temporary signs are those that fade fairly quickly. A footprint in the grass is a good example of a temporary sign.

Permanent signs are those that last for a long time (several weeks) or will never disappear. Broken twigs, scraped bark, and displaced soil are just a few examples of permanent signs.

Remember that as you track someone you will likely see them leave the same type of signs repeatedly. This is because people tend to be careless over and over in the same fashion. It becomes their habit. It doesn't mean that they are trying to leave signs for you to see, it means that they aren't thinking and are not aware of what they are doing. If you are lucky enough to detect the same signs over and over, don't neglect to keep looking for other types of signs. Sooner or later you will likely see them as well.

Tracking Indicators

There are a number of basic signs, or tracking indicators. They are displacement, litter, stains, weathering, and camouflage. You may see only one or two of these signs as you track someone or you may see all of them. It just depends on the situation and the amount of signs a person leaves as he moves through an area.

Displacement

This is when anything is moved from its original position. When someone steps on soft or moist ground and leaves a well-defined footprint, it is a good example of the displacement of the soil that was moved to form the imprint. The imprint left by the weight and compression of his foot displaced the soil in such a way as to leave a sign he had been there. By studying this sign you can gain a good deal of information about the individual who left it, such as his approximate size, direction of movement, and condition of footgear.

Displacement can be the result of someone breaking through dense vegetation or cutting a trail through thick underbrush. This type of displacement is difficult to miss even for the inexperienced tracker. Displacement can also be caused by someone carrying a large, heavy pack or weapons that may become caught on vegetation. Signs of displacement may be made when someone stops to rest and sets the equipment he's carrying down on the ground. This causes the ground and the vegetation to become displaced by the weight. When someone lies down he causes grass to be bent and twigs to become broken. This type of displacement can be missed if you aren't observant.

As you track someone, you may find a point in the trail where there are a series of good displacement footprints that you can examine in sequence. This will likely give you a great deal of information regarding the person or persons you are following. If the prints are deep and the stride is unusually long it is a good indicator that the person is running or moving rapidly. Usually the toe prints will be deeper than the heel if he is running and pushing off and down with the toe. On the other hand, if the prints are deep, widely spaced, and short, with the ground disturbed as though he was shuffling, then this is an indication that he may have been carrying a very heavy load or may be injured or extremely tired.

You may come across someone who attempts to throw you off the trail by walking backward. This rarely works and is easily spotted by a good tracker. Walking backward is difficult to do under the best of circumstances and can be particularly difficult in a rural environment. As a result, his tracks will be shorter than normal and his stride will be irregular. The most telling signs are that his footprint has an unnaturally deep toe mark and the soil is displaced in the direction of the movement. It will also likely show that he dragged his heel in the direction of his movement.

A clear displacement sign may allow you to determine the sex of the person who made the print. This can be determined by examining the size and position of the print. In most cases women tend to walk with their toes pointed slightly inward while men walk with their feet straight ahead or pointed slightly to the outside. Also, prints left by women are usually smaller and their stride is normally shorter than a man's.

When a group of people moves through an area, the last person leaves the clearest footprints. As a result, these become the key prints to follow. You can cut a stick to match the distance between the prints. When you measure the distance of the prints you can measure it from heel to heel or toe to toe. It is important that you measure the same way each time to remain consistent and avoid confusion. You should also notch the stick with the width of the print to aid in finding a partial print.

A good tracker observes for distinguishing traits when he has a clear displacement print. The trait may be anything that sets the print apart from others such as a distinguishing sole pattern, a unique mark, or the indication of frayed or worn footgear. If the trail becomes difficult to see or follow, the tracker can then employ this stick to find hard-to-see prints. This will aid him to identify where the next prints should be, and he can examine this area closer for signs of those he is tracking. Knowing where the prints should be and knowing a distinct sign associated with a print will make it easier to determine where the tracks will lead.

There are a number of other types of displacement signs you can look for. Foliage, rocks, sticks, moss, and vines that are displaced can alert you to the direction to follow. One of the best displacement signs is when one or more people step across a fallen tree and scrape some of the bark off the log. People traveling with heavy, bulky equipment often create displacement signs by scuffing the bark of a tree they pass. Stepping on exposed roots also displaces the bark; this is an excellent sign that will remain for a long time. When dirt, mud, or other ground debris is moved there are signs of displacement, such as broken dirt seals around rocks. When stones or sticks on the ground have been recently overturned they will be a different color from others in the area due to the effects of weathering. Other good signs of displacement are may be disturbed anthills, spider webs, and other insect or animal nests.

Signs of displacement can also come from those you are following. Any good tracker is constantly on the lookout for bits of clothing or threads left by those who moved through the area earlier. People tend to drop things or let their clothing get snagged on thorns and briars when moving through dense foliage and rugged terrain. When crossing roads or streams, tracks are left and soil is transferred from one area to another. If a person tries to move through a stream to cover his trail he is likely to disturb rocks and algae. Entering and leaving the stream produces displacement marks such as footprints and slide marks. These are all good signs of displacement that can aid you as a tracker. Keep in mind that people will take the path of least resistance, which means they are going to move in the direction that has the least vegetation and is easiest to walk on. Use this knowledge to assist you in looking for tracks.

Stains

These are another sign that can help you track your quarry. One of the best examples of a stain is blood from a wounded subject. Bloodstains may appear as drops or spatters, depending on the size and location of the wound. It is important to keep in mind that bloodstains may not always appear on the ground; they may appear on leaves or other vegetation and could be smeared where a person has leaned against or touched something.

The seriousness of the wound can sometimes be determined by the amount of blood and by the distance that has been traveled by the wounded person. If a pattern develops in the way the bloodstains appear along the trail, it may be possible to estimate where the wound is on the individual. For example, if the stains indicate that the blood is dripping steadily, the wound is likely coming from a wound to the trunk. If the blood appears to be slung to the front and rear or to the sides, it may be coming from wounds to one or more of the limbs. If it is consistently slung off to the side it is very likely that it is coming from one or both arms as he swings them while moving.

Blood patterns, amounts, and color may also indicate how serious the wound is and how profuse the bleeding may be. When an arterial wound is involved, the bloodstain may be at regular intervals, while a wound to the vein would be steadier. Blood from a wound to the lung would appear pink, bubbly, and frothy as a result of the air and blood mixing in the lungs. If the wound is from the head, a great deal of staining on vegetation both on the ground and above the knees is likely. (Blood from a head wound appears heavy and slimy.) An abdominal wound bloodstain may contain blood mixed with digestive juices; there would be a distinctive odor and it would appear light in color. Other body fluids such as sweat, urine, or feces can also help the tracker. Whether left on the ground, rocks, bushes, or trees, these substances are likely to leave a stain. When conditions are dry or dusty people may spit or sneeze, leaving signs or stains from these as well.

Staining can also take place when someone steps on grass or leaves that may leave a chlorophyll stain on a limb or rock. A stone or root can be stained when leaves or berries are crushed against it by someone walking through the area.

On days when there is little or no wind and the sun is shining, the normal position of leaves on plants is dark side up. When a person passes by and disturbs these leaves some of them may turn upside down, showing their lighter side, and will remain in that position for some time. This is called a flag, and if you have ever observed it you will understand why. This flag can often be seen from a distance, allowing you to see the trail extend a long distance. This discoloration may also be referred to by some as "shine." Grass and live leaves that are stepped on will often be bruised on this lighter side and may leave a stain, depending on what material is under them. Leaves or grass may leave a stain on rocks or hard ground that might otherwise not reveal a track.

Weathering

This is the effect the elements have on any tracks or signs that have been left. This can come from one or more aspects of weather such as rain, sunlight, wind, temperature, snow, or any other influence. It takes time and experience to know and understand how the weather can affect signs.

Weathering can have a dramatic affect on footprints. What may have been a perfectly clear print can become almost invisible or partially destroyed depending on several factors. For example, if the soil is loose and sandy and is exposed to direct wind and sun, the print will not last as long as it might if the weather were not directly affecting it. But sometimes weathering can aid a tracker. An example of this is when a footprint is found in a muddy area where it has rained and the sun has baked the print into the ground. When a footprint is observed and the particles of soil around the edges are just beginning to fall into the print, the print is very fresh and the tracker should use extreme caution. On the other hand,

if the edges of the footprint are beginning to dry and become crusty, the print is probably more than an hour old. These are only general guidelines and are dependent on the terrain and such factors as temperature and humidity.

It is important for trackers to be aware of what the weather in the area has been for the previous several days in order to make a realistic assessment of the age of a trail. A light rain may only round off the edges of a footprint, whereas a heavy rain could wash out prints completely.

As mentioned earlier, wind can have a dramatic affect on tracks and signs. Leaves that turn over because someone brushes against them could return to their original position if it gets windy. Wind can also blow debris into footprints and may even cause some prints to be masked by debris. It is important for the tracker to recall the wind activity in the area if he is to estimate the age of a track.

Wind can also directly affect sounds and odors. If the wind is blowing toward the tracker from the direction of the person he is following it can carry sounds and odors to him, but if the tracker is upwind he must be very cautious since the wind may carry the sounds he makes toward the person he is tracking. It is sometimes difficult to determine which way the wind is blowing. You can determine the wind direction by taking a handful of dirt or debris and slowly dropping it from shoulder height to see which way it blows. Keep in mind that the wind can frequently change, so it is wise to check the direction frequently.

Another thing to keep in mind is that temperature and time of day determine the way the wind moves and whether there is any wind at all. For example, during the middle of the day when it is warmer the wind may not be moving at all, but later in the day it can become windier. Temperature can also affect which way the wind may move. As the sun warms the air in low-lying areas the air moves uphill, and as the air cools in the evening it moves back into lower areas. This is good to remember if you are following someone in mountainous terrain. As you track someone or move into a position for a rural surveillance operation, keep in mind the direction of the wind and try to use it to your advantage.

Litter

This is anything that does not belong in the area where the track is. I recently saw a clump of pine needles lying along a trail I was following in a hardwood forest. They stood out because there were no pine trees within several hundred yards. I later learned that one of the people we were following had used clumps of pine branches to break the outline of his hat. It was a good idea but he failed to secure the camouflage to his headgear and it helped us follow him. Every time you look at something that catches your eye, ask yourself if it really belongs in the area; if it draws your attention there is a strong possibility that it does not.

Some of the most obvious types of litter are candy or food wrappers, cigarette butts, urine or feces, remains of fires, shreds of clothing, and pieces of equipment. Many times you will find pieces of cloth left from someone tearing his clothing on vegetation. Weather has an affect on litter and may wash some of it away or destroy it. The weathering of litter can also tell you how long ago someone left it there. It is important that rural surveillance teams carry out everything they bring, including litter, so there is no sign you were in the area.

Camouflage

In this context it applies to someone who is being tracked attempting to lose those who are tracking him. A person may or may not know that he is being tracked but may attempt to camouflage his trail as a precaution. Any good rural surveillance team should attempt to do this when moving to or away from its target. If you are tracking someone or following a trail and you see indications that he is attempting to use camouflage to hide his trail, you should use extreme caution and make sure that your security is on the highest alert.

Some of the techniques used by people to hide their trail are to walk backward to a certain point and then move off in another direction. Another technique is to leave several trails to confuse the tracking team. Someone using camouflage may try to brush out his trail, leaving no distinguishing prints in the immediate area. Moving over rocky terrain or traveling for some distance through a stream are other methods that may be employed to lose a tracker. If you discover that one or more of these techniques are being employed, use caution. It may take you some time to relocate and begin following the true trail, but remember that the person who worked to cover his tracks also lost time doing so.

Dogs and Trackers

This chapter would not be complete if it didn't address the use of dogs and how they can aid in tracking. The myths and inaccurate information that surround tracking dogs and their capabilities are legion. Every time a dog is seen in the movies or on television tracking someone or something people believe that a dog can track anything. What most people fail to realize is that the dog or dogs are only one part of a team. The other critical part of that team is the handler of the dogs doing the tracking.

Canine tracking involves the merging of the talents of both the man and the dog. As a man-and-dog tracking team works to follow someone the dog is using its senses of hearing, smell, and sight. The man is using his sight as well as his understanding of what the quarry might be doing. When you combine the talents of the dog and the man, it can be quite formidable.

Just as a good tracker is a rare and difficult asset to replace, the same is true of a good tracking dog. The visual tracker often helps the dog or his handlers find the trail in the event it is lost by the dog. Although a visual tracker may be slower than the dogs and tire more quickly, his ability to think and reason concerning what the quarry may do is invaluable. Years ago I was working on the Survival Committee at Fort Bragg, North Carolina. We were tracking people with the assistance of a tracker and his dogs that were often used by the North Carolina Department of Corrections when convicts would escape.

These particular dogs had an impressive record of locating escapees, and I asked their handler what was the best technique for escaping when dogs were tracking you. I'll never forget his answer: "Unless the conditions are in your favor you ain't gonna beat the dog's nose; you have to beat the dog's handler."

A misconception about tracking dogs is that once they get a person's scent, they are able to follow it directly to the person. This is just not so. In fact, during a hunt for a human, dogs may lose the scent many times and sometimes may not relocate it. Just as weather can affect the tracks left by someone traveling through an area, weather can also destroy the scent. Scent is short-lived and how long it may last is dependent on a number of factors, including the ground it was left on as well as the weather. Depending on the strength of the ground wind, airborne scents can be blown away almost as soon as they are left or they may remain for hours. Ground scents can last for up to two days if conditions are favorable.

Light rain or drizzle along with ground fog that keeps the ground moist are ideal for holding a scent to the ground for a long period, but too much hard rain can wash a scent away. In most cases, however, a scent is just washed into the ground and sealed beneath a layer of groundwater. Many people believe that a short, hard rain will wash a scent trail away, but this isn't the case. What really occurs is that the water may seal in the scent and, as the area begins to dry, the ground releases the scent again and a tracking dog can pick up the trail.

While tracking dogs are mainly scent hunters, many of them also can use their short-range vision to follow a trail. One distinct advantage they have is they see the trail from a different angle than their handler or a tracker and so may see tracks that a person might miss. One disadvantage a dog has is colorblindness. Dogs also do not have good long-range vision and are very poor at detecting something that is well camouflaged. This is good to know if you are conducting a surveillance operation against a target and there are dogs in the area.

They can however, detect slight movements much better than a human can. This is why it is critical to remain absolutely still if a dog is near your hide site. A dog also has an incredible sense of hearing and can hear sounds far beyond what the human ear is capable of detecting. Unknown to most people is the fact that a dog will use its ability to smell to get to the general area of a person and will then rely on its hearing and movement detection to pinpoint the target.

Dogs and dog tracker teams also have limitations and weaknesses. The most apparent and exploitable is that of defeating the tracker. If the tracker or handler is not in good physical condition, that may be your biggest advantage. Also, following a scent is hard work for a dog. The effort they put into it is so intense that they are not able to keep doing it for long periods without a break. As a general rule, dogs and their handlers work a trail for about a half-hour before the dog needs a rest. But they can't do this indefinitely. Their efficiency begins to significantly decrease as the hunt wears on, and it is often necessary to bring in a new dog and handler as time passes.

As a member of a rural surveillance that may encounter dogs, it is important to know how to prevent them from following or detecting you. Likewise, if you use dogs to assist you it is important to know their limitations. The best defense against a dog in the area (other than a weapon with a silencer) is good camouflage along with light, noise, and trash discipline. Dogs will locate a team by discovering a trail or by detecting human waste odors from a hide site or a base camp. This is why it is so critical to limit and obscure trails around campsites. Many dog-tracker teams first locate signs of their quarry by walking roads and wood lines searching for trails left by that person. The following are some things to consider doing if you think you may be working against a dog and tracker team.

- Minimize your tracks and approach your base camp or hide site over dry, hard ground or rock.

- Maintain noise and light discipline at all times during an operation.
- Never smoke during an operation.
- Double wrap all trash in plastic bags and carry it out of the area when you leave.
- Urinate in a hole and cover it up. Urinate in a different spot each time.
- Bury fecal matter in a deep hole or put in sealed bags to take out when you leave.
- Take up a position as far away from the target as you can that still allows you to conduct your mission.
- Try to remain downwind from the dogs if at all possible.

COUNTERTRACKING

One of the first things a military sniper may do to counter a tracker or a tracking team is to initially travel away from his intended target. This is a good practice to employ for a rural surveillance operation if the terrain and situation allow for it. Evading an experienced tracker or an experienced dog-tracker team is extremely difficult at best. During a rural surveillance operation, many times you will be working in an area where the subject of your surveillance knows the area very well and may be highly aware of any changes in the area. If you are going to remain undetected or defeat someone who may be tracking you, it is critical that you have a plan to avoid detection and practice techniques prior to an actual operation. The following are techniques used by some military units to avoid being followed.

Cutting the corner is a technique that is employed when approaching a known road or trail. At a distance of 100 to 200 meters before reaching the road, the team turns 45 degrees right or left away from the direction it plans to follow. The team comes out on the road and travels along the side of the road or trail leaving good tracks for the tracker to follow. After a distance of a few hundred meters, the team backtracks to the point where it entered the road and then carefully moves off in the direction it initially planned to go. This technique is to make the tracker believe those

he was following got lazy and used the road or trail to move faster. This will not usually fool an experienced tracker but it will cause him some delay and could cause him to believe the team may have split up.

Walking backward is one of the basic techniques discussed earlier in the chapter. This trick will not often fool an experienced tracker, so it must be done with great care if it is to be successful. When walking backward, you must take time to step lightly so as to give the appearance that you were only in the track once. It is important not to put too much pressure on any one part of your foot and not to drag your heel as you step away from the track. To employ this technique properly takes time and skill and it can't be accomplished in a hurry.

Large tree is a deception technique in which you change direction at large trees. To do this you move 10 to 20 paces past a large tree in the wrong direction. You then carefully and slowly walk backward to the forward side of the tree and make a change of 90 degrees in the direction you want to travel. This technique is designed to utilize the tree as a type of screen to mask your new trail from someone who may be tracking you. A variation to this technique is to use a clear area to help deceive the tracker. With this technique you travel past a large tree located near an open field. Walking past the tree you continue into the field for at least 100 meters and reenter the wood line. It is important that you try to leave a clear trail as you are doing this. Once you have walked several meters into the woods, you halt and carefully walk backward to the tree, taking time to ensure that you do not leave signs of what you have done. At the tree you step off behind the tree and move off in your new direction. Again, the tree is utilized to mask your new trail. Keep in mind that this will take time and may not work against an experienced tracker.

Slip the stream is a countertracking ploy you may want to use when approaching a stream. As in the technique of cutting the corner you approach the stream at a 45-degree angle, entering the stream and traveling upstream for some distance. Depending on the time you have available, you can establish several false trails either on one or both sides of the stream, making sure that none of the false trails heads in the direction your intend to actually travel. Following this, you reverse direction and move downstream, well past the location you entered and carefully exit in the direction you wish to continue traveling. (The reason for traveling upstream first, away from the direction of your intended travel, is to prevent any floating debris or dirt to compromise your actual direction of travel.)

Fishhook is a great little tactic that is extremely effective if used properly. This is used by a team or individual to double back and set up in a position that allows them to view the trail they previously traveled. The most important part of this countertracking tactic is that it must be done in terrain and vegetation that can mask your movement and provide a vantage point where you can safely observe the area you just traveled through.

These techniques can be employed by you and your team but they can also be used against you, so you need to always be alert.

You need to practice these techniques as a team. Waiting to employ them when it's the real thing can lead to some nasty surprises and you may fail. Also remember that trackers and dogs are not infallible. They can make mistakes and get confused.

Whether you are tracking someone or trying to avoid being tracked yourself, it is important to understand the fundamentals of tracking and how difficult it may be to track someone. As mentioned earlier, tracking and countertracking are skills you must practice to become proficient. When training as a team, you should include tracking as part of your training every time you have the opportunity. Have half the team track the other half and then switch roles. The competition will make the training more realistic, and you will quickly discover your strengths and weaknesses. Remember that this is an area you need to be strong in. Understanding tracking and countertracking techniques can save the team and help you successfully accomplish your mission.

Chapter Nine:
Target Surveillance and Intelligence Collection

Conducting surveillance and collecting intelligence on the target and its inhabitants is the ultimate goal of any rural surveillance operation. Whether it is for a few hours or for several days or more, the ultimate goal is to remain undetected and to accomplish your objective. Once on the target, it becomes painfully clear how important many of the previously discussed subjects are.

It also becomes clear how critical it is that the purpose of the operation is clearly defined. Once on the target you may find that the situation has changed and the purpose of the surveillance has changed as well. But in the beginning of the actual surveillance, clearly establishing your objectives is critical.

As you move into the target area and conduct your initial reconnaissance it becomes clear that the ultimate objective of your operation will determine, in large part, where you will base your operation and how you may have to organize an extended operation. What is your ultimate objective and can you accomplish it without compromising your team and the mission?

Once team members select hide sites from which they will collect information, it is important that they continue to evaluate the site to ensure that it provides them with the concealment they need. It is often the case that a team sets up to observe activity on a target and they become so focused on the target that they forget about checking their own security. As time passes and night turns into day or the position of the sun changes and casts light in a different way, the surveillance teams need to constantly check that others can't detect them. The success of the operation requires that you remain focused on your safety and concealment as well as on the target you are closely observing.

Whether your mission objective is to determine what activities are taking place in the target area or to collect information to plan a raid on the target, it is necessary to get as much detailed information as possible. To do this, you must approach your mission with the attitude that everything you observe in and around the target area is important. You can never gather too much information on a target. When I teach this course to students and one of them asks me what I want to know about a target my response is always the same—EVERYTHING!

Your approach should be to observe and record what takes place to the extent that you can paint a very clear, chronological picture to those you brief when your operation is completed. Your goal is to paint a clear picture in the minds of all those who attend the briefing. Your records should be in such detail as to withstand questioning during a trial if you are later called to testify about what you saw.

To conduct accurate observations, it is important to understand the basic techniques of observation. On a rural surveillance operation the team members in the hide site observing the target are the eyes and ears of the operation. They must be "switched on" and employing all of their senses. The operators must be able to observe and collect detailed information whether in a daylight or nighttime environment. One of the biggest mistakes some operators make is trying to get too close instead of employing the optical devices available to them. If you get too close and the conditions change, you could be trapped or exposed.

NIGHT SURVEILLANCE

As more teams become better trained and capable, night operations are being used more frequently to collect intelligence. In many circumstances, operating at night can greatly increase the chances of success and lower the risks of being detected. However, teams may need to establish a surveillance operation that runs for several days and requires them to observe the target continuously, under both night and daylight conditions.

To be successful during hours of darkness or periods of limited visibility, it is important to understand how the human eye works and its capabilities and limitations. The eyes are made up of cone cells and rod cells and each serves a distinct purpose for vision. The cone cells help us determine colors, shapes, and sharp contrasts of objects we observe. They require a good deal of sunlight or a very good light source during the hours of darkness. If lighting is poor, such as the light given off by a low-power porch light, you may have trouble determining the color of a car or the identity of a person. The rod cells of the human eye have a pigment called visual purple that allows them to see during periods of darkness or low illumination. Some people have better vision at night than others. As people age this ability usually weakens.

During darkness or periods of limited lighting, it usually takes about 30 seconds for the human eye to get to the point where it can fully distinguish objects. During this period, the pupils of the eyes are expanding to take in more available light. More than one person has temporarily lost the ability to see when a light went off or one was suddenly turned on, causing him to lose his night vision. It may be during this time that the most important activity on the target takes place, and loss of your night vision, if only for a moment, can cause you to miss an opportunity to collect valuable information. This is why you need to be ready to protect your eyes at night from a sudden bright light.

One of the best ways to observe at night is to employ a technique called off-center vision. This technique works by looking to one side of an object rather than straight at it. The reason this technique works at night is because direct vision by the human eye requires the use of cones. By looking to either side of an object or just below or above it, the image is formed by the rod cells, where the eyes are most sensitive in darkness. You are basically looking at an object and seeing it out of the corner of your eye with more clarity and definition than if you were to look at it directly during darkness. This works best when you look approximately 10 degrees off from the object you are trying to observe. Using this technique to look off-center works for most people, but the image your eye holds will not remain consistent. Usually, after about 10 to 15 seconds the image will fade into the background unless you have exceptionally strong night vision.

Scanning is a little trick you can use to keep an object in view while at the same time strengthening your off-center vision. By shifting the point where you are looking from one area to another, you can continue to maintain the image in view. Irregular movements from one point near the object or person to another helps to move the image within your eyes and different eye cells are used, preventing the image from fading.

Factors Affecting Night Vision

It is vital to know what factors can adversely affect your night vision. Some of these factors can be controlled and others cannot, but any one of them can lead to the failure of a rural surveillance operation. An operator who has a head cold, a headache, fatigue, smokes heavily, or uses alcohol to excess can experience a reduced ability to see during darkness. A diet that does not provide enough vitamin A can also impair a person's night vision and taking mega doses of vitamin A will not immediately fix the problem. Being exposed to a bright light while working in darkness will temporarily blind you and it will take several minutes to regain your night vision. Since darkness eliminates or distorts detail and color it is important to be able to recognize objects by their outline. This can't always be reliable but can be helpful in many situations.

One of the most difficult times to see things clearly is during twilight. As light changes and begins to diminish, you have to start making adjustments to see certain things. Twilight is also a time when a sense of urgency or false security begins to set in. I have often seen teams try to move closer to a target before it becomes completely dark, feeling that they are concealed by the approaching darkness. They will move in closer before dark because they want to be able to see where they are moving before all light is gone. This can be a fatal mistake and can compromise the entire operation. Also, twilight can be a time when there may be increased activity on a target, especially during the warmer times of the year. People tend to stay outside during and past the twilight hours, and this increased activity can put a team at risk, especially if the team tries to move before activity in the target area settles down. Because light changes constantly during twilight, the eyes will have to adjust and this may limit your power to observe activity or a threat in the area. Whenever possible, wait until it is dark and your night vision is adjusted before moving near the target area.

OBSERVATION AIDS

Binoculars

There is a wide selection of observation aids on the market today; some are excellent and some are poor. Binoculars are the most obvious and versatile aid, and no team member should be without a good pair. In fact, I recommend that each team member carry a good backup set of binoculars just in case his first pair becomes lost or damaged.

Most binoculars use a magnification of 7x in a 50mm objective lens. There are different types and you may want to experiment with which power and magnification works best for you. I have used a number of different types and sizes and I have found that you get what you pay for in terms of quality. Buying a cheap pair of binoculars may save you a few dollars but it can cause you to miss collecting vital information about a target.

Spotter Scopes

Every rural surveillance team should have a spotter scope as part of its equipment. Most of the spotter scopes have an increased power and magnification of 20 to 50x and can detect objects over greater distances as long as there is sufficient light available. Because of the increased power and distances involved, these scopes have to be very stable when viewing an object; some can be mounted on small tripods for looking at targets at long distances.

A spotter scope is an excellent item to have in a hide site if you observe an object and you aren't quite sure what it is. With a

The use of good optic equipment can ensure the detailed collection of critical mission intelligence. Quality scopes and binoculars can allow you to dramatically increase the detail of the information you gather.

powerful spotter scope, you can take a closer look and possibly identify the object. You can purchase good spotter scopes at most sporting goods stores.

I have seen some clever operators use sniper/rifle scopes to aid them as well. As with any scope or set of binoculars, be sure you use some type of cover or netting to prevent a reflection off the scope from giving your position away.

Night Vision

Night-vision goggles (NVGs) are great and can provide a significant boost to a surveillance operation during the hours of darkness. Even the older generation of NVGs can be useful and help avoid eyestrain at night. They do have limitations and take some getting used to, so it is important that the operators become familiar with them before taking them on an actual operation. If your team has NVGs it needs to practice using and moving with them often. Keep in mind that, like any piece of equipment, they can break and for this reason a team should never get into the habit of depending on them too much.

TYPES OF SEARCHES

There are two types of searches you can conduct during a surveillance of a target. One is a hasty search and the other is a detailed search.

Hasty Search

A hasty search is conducted immediately as you move into an area to set up a base camp, stop to rest while moving, or move into the target area to set up a hide site. A hasty search is conducted over an entire area and is designed to discover any immediate danger. A hasty search can be made with the aid of binoculars if necessary, using quick glances at specific points throughout the area. A hasty search is not supposed to be used to take in a large panoramic view of an area, rather, it is a quick glance to gain information about the immediate and surrounding areas. The hasty search relies on the eye's sensitivity to movement or anything that seems out of place in a particular area.

Detailed Search

A detailed search takes more time and looks at things in more detail. This is the type of search an operator would employ when he feels he is reasonably secure and may be well concealed. A detailed search is conducted on a target and the target area when a surveillance team is looking for a hide site or when the team is in the hide site and observing the target.

During the detailed search it is important to cover the entire surrounding area. One of the best ways to do this is to break up the area into different sectors and search each sector in detail. This kind of methodical search helps make sure that you haven't missed any one area. Searching by sector also helps you to concentrate on the details of items and areas within a sector, which in turn causes you to look much more closely at particular items within those areas. It is important to overlap each sector or area so you don't miss anything.

Snipers often overlap each area by 30 to 50 meters. This technique is referred to as the overlapping-strip method and guarantees that no area is missed. I strongly recommend this.

During a detailed search, if an item is spotted and a positive identification cannot be made, then the rifle or spotter scope should be employed. Once the entire area has been searched, use binoculars to periodically check the area. It is a good idea to have each person in the hide site make checks just to have more than one set of eyes looking over the area and to reduce fatigue.

RECORDING TARGET INFORMATION

Following the first detailed search of the target and the surrounding area, it is imperative that the teams begin recording details. One of the most important and often overlooked items is the orientation of sketches and descriptions of the target. I can't begin to recall how many times I have seen teams give a briefing on the results of surveillance operations using good sketches of targets without having them oriented to any reference point.

I can remember one briefing where a team had a target under surveillance for more than 24 hours and had captured every detail and activity about the target. About halfway through the briefing, they were asked which direction the front of the house was facing and the only reference they could give was that it was "kinda facing towards the railroad tracks." "Kinda facing" is not a very specific direction or orientation. In fact, if you were to return to the target, which had several buildings, you might not know which was the building in question.

Since more than one team member is involved in collecting information on a target, and this information is going to be combined to hopefully provide complete coverage of a target and its surrounding area, all members should orient themselves in the same way. The best way is for everyone to orient on magnetic north. Each member already has a compass, so it is easy enough for all of them to mark north on all their sketches of the target. Also, once they are on the target, each member should be orienting his sketches and written records with the compass, so if he needs to record the direction in which someone went or came from he would be able to do so.

It is absolutely essential that your team SOP cover how you are going to orient your sketches and that your team trains this way. Any good rural surveillance team will incorporate sketching into its training to ensure the information it collects on a target is going to be useful to anyone who needs it.

Structures

Almost every target you put under surveillance will consist of one or more structures. (A typical exception is a plot of land used to grow marijuana.) Almost all surveillances I have been involved with had more than one structure, even if one was nothing more than a shed or a carport. Even though the target may be one specific building, you still must collect all the information you can about other buildings in the immediate area. A barn or toolshed next to your target building may one day be the actual target. You may have an entire compound consisting of multiple buildings, none of which can be determined to be the primary target, and you will need to sketch and collect information on all of them. To do a thorough job you need to use a format to ensure that you don't miss anything.

Identification

The first thing to do when sketching and describing a structure is to establish some identification. Be as specific and accurate as you can. Often a building has an address or a number on it that makes it unique and sets it apart from other nearby buildings. It may have a sign on it or pointing to it that states what building it is, such as the administration building or utility building. If there is an official name or local name use that as one way of identifying each structure, but always use a second means of identification. You may want to identify a building by its functional description such as calling it the storage building, pump house, or toolshed. Another way to identify a structure is by giving its general location, such as "north of the bridge." If the structure is on a map you can use map references as well as grid coordinates. On your sketches and descriptions of structures, the use of azimuths and distances are a very good way to help establish which structure you are describing, but you must be very accurate when using this method. The azimuths and distances must be recorded in relation to predominant terrain features that can be referenced and that will not likely change in the future.

Grounds Description

The immediate grounds and the surrounding area are of great importance during a rural surveillance. A good sketch along with a detailed written description should be initiated as soon as the team gets a view of the area. This description needs to continue to be developed as the team has more time to study the area and collect more detailed information.

All fencing should be part of the description and as much detail as possible must be included. Whether the fencing is anchored or loose along the grounds, the material it is made of, and the location and types of gates or openings in the fencing are all-important items to include in your report. Even if there is fencing other than that defining the perimeter, it should be recorded in detail.

All entrances to the target area should be recorded, whether they are main roads or just footpaths.

All structures in the area need to be a major part of the grounds description, which should also include a detailed section covering the terrain and vegetation in and around the target area. This information is vital. A good detail of the terrain will be needed if a raid is going to be planned for the future. The slope of the land and description of vegetation may dictate the location of future hide sites if another surveillance is planned. It is very important to give as much detail and to include the time of year and type of vegetation observed.

Any additional information not covered above needs to be included in the description of the target grounds. During the final, detailed observation of the grounds it is of great importance not to miss a single detail. Items such as an old cement block in the yard or garden tools lying about can be of importance later when a team member has to move through the area during darkness. Nothing should be left out of the description of the grounds if the team observes it.

Building Descriptions

Exteriors

When describing any buildings, it is recommended to first begin by giving a thorough description of the exterior. Describe what the building is made of, its color, foundation, and whether anything is attached or built on to it. Record the locations of the drainpipes, power boxes, air conditioners, windows, railings or anything else that makes up the building's exterior. One team's members, believing the side of a building was solid, had a rude awaking during a raid attempt when they discovered that it was in fact made of corrugated metal that gave away their presence when they bumped against it in the dark.

Building Entrances

If there is a main entrance to the building it should be designated as such and described in detail. If possible, make a sketch and photo of each entrance. Even entrances that are not used or appear to be blocked need to be described in detail. Likewise, any emergency entrances and exits should be described in detail and their locations recorded. Make sure to report: the type of locks on the entrances along with the direction the door opens and closes; the type of doorframe; sliding glass doors and the

direction they open; and the estimated thickness of the glass. There is no information about the entrances that is too small or insignificant to be mentioned.

Interior Description of Buildings

Although rural surveillance team members may not be able to gain access to the interior of a building in a target area, there is a great deal of information they can collect about the interior if they are patient and observant. A great deal of information can often be gained at night when the interior lights are on and part of the interior can be observed from the outside. Even when shades are drawn and there is no clear view into the interior, lights going on and off and sounds from inside can give the team a good idea of what activities are taking place and which rooms are which. (For example, if a light goes on in a room and you hear a washing machine or dryer start up, you have a pretty good idea that area is the wash area. Or if a light goes on in a room with a smaller window, possibly with frosted glass, and you hear a toilet flush or a shower running, it's a safe bet that that's a bathroom.)

Over time, by watching the activities, noting the times lights go on and off, listening, and getting glimpses through opened windows and doors, you can piece together a basic layout of a residence or other structure. Most residential structures, whether they are mobile homes or permanently built structures, have a predictable layout. The time it was constructed and location of the home can also serve to help determine the interior layout. For example, a home built prior to World War II may be laid out much differently than one of the many homes built following the war. Old homes built in the country as large farmhouses often had washrooms in the back of the house off the kitchen area and possibly a basement storage area that can only be accessed from the outside of the house. Understanding the types of homes that exist in the area you are operating in and how they were constructed can help you to determine how the interior of the building is set up.

If the building is a large one with no way of seeing into it from the outside, you may be able to determine its interior layout by obtaining copies from official or unofficial sources such as the fire department, health department, or the company that designed or built it. You may also want to consider if there is anyone with access to the target that might be willing to work as an informant. His or her motivation needs to be closely examined, and this should be considered as a last result.

You will want to create an overall floor plan for each floor; to do so you need to attempt to determine where interior corridors lead, whether there is more than one floor or a basement, and where the stairways are that lead to them.

If you are conducting surveillance on a large building or a complex of buildings, one or more of the buildings may have elevators. Elevators require inspections and maintenance, and these records are a good source of information for the location of the elevators as well as other things. A rooftop door used to maintain the elevator may reveal the existence of elevators in the building.

Record the location of windows and the types of locks on them. Even if the windows are blocked or appear to have furniture pushed up against them from the inside, you must record as much detail as possible. Just as with a door you should note the type and condition of the window frame; if there is a screen or storm window over a regular window, this should be noted on your sketch and in your target report. At night, if any light shows through the window, this could be useful information and should be noted.

Physical barriers you may observe, such as railings inside a large building or chairs and tables inside a home or office, should be noted. If they are later moved or missing, this should also be reported. Any areas in the interior that appear to have had extra work completed on them that may have been added after the regular construction, such as reinforced doors or the hardening of a particular area, should be noted and reported to the team leader. The reinforcement of structures, particularly residential structures, may be indications of drug or militia activity. Anything else that can be observed of the interior of a target building needs to be noted and recorded particularly if there is the possibility that the target could be raided in the future. There is no item that should be considered insignificant if it is observed inside a target or potential target structure.

The description of the roofs is also important and can provide valuable information. Teams often don't bother to gather detailed information about roofs because they don't think about them. However a roof may have entrances and exits, fire escapes, ladders, and elevator rooms. They also can serve as excellent secure locations to observe anyone operating in the area around them. If you are involved in an operation against a potentially high threat, get a good look at the roof areas before moving in closer. Look for anything such as chairs, sandbags, or trash (food wrappers and drink cans) that indicate the roof is occupied at times.

Systems
Power
One of the most important areas to fully investigate is the power supply and systems. What is the normal source of power and is there a backup system? Are the power meter and the power lines leading into the facility above or below ground?

The company that provides power to the facility can be a great source of information, such as the rate of power use at different times of year, and may also have information that is not necessarily related just to the power—such as the layout of the facility. If the target provides its own power, how is it generated and how vulnerable is it? If a raid needs to be planned, this will become an important issue.

Lighting
Lighting can tell a great deal about the target. It can be a threat to you but, as mentioned earlier, the shadows it casts can also aid you in collecting information about the target. Indoor lighting can help you to gain information at night about what is inside a structure and may tell you what the structure is used for. Outside lighting can help you to identify activities taking place as well as help identify individuals and vehicles in the area during darkness. You will need to report all inside and outside lighting. If you are collecting data on the target for an extended period, you should report the times when lights are used and when they are off. The

location and brightness of security lighting also needs to be reported. Of equal importance is to determine where the lighting does not exist and the shadows that are cast. Also be looking for any emergency lighting that may be installed and record its locations as well.

Water

This is a critical source for any facility and you need to determine the source during your surveillance. Just as with the power systems, you will want to determine if there is a backup source for water such as a nearby stream or a well. You should also be alert to see if there is any indication of efforts to store water. Based upon the activities taking place in the target area, try to determine if water is a critical requirement for those activities. Also, look for any holding tanks and aboveground pipes leading into buildings. This may help you determine the activities and purpose of certain structures.

Food

When observing a target for more than a few hours, you will likely have the opportunity to determine how people at the target get their meals. It is important to note if they go out to eat, if someone brings food to them, or if they have the ability to fix it there. Also try to determine if they store food supplies that would allow them to go for a period without being resupplied. Related to this, determining how people at the target get rid of garbage can be a great source of intelligence. Is it dumped on or near the target or off site? (Garbage should only be searched if it will not expose the team or the operation.)

Fire Protection

This may appear to be an unlikely subject to address, but information about fire protection or the lack of it can reveal a good deal of information about a target. For example, are there any flammables used and stored in the area? Is there a fuel storage area and is there firefighting equipment available? If so, why? Has a fire inspection ever been conducted? This is another potential source of information, as well as an opportunity to gain inside access. Are there any indications of hazardous materials being used or stored in

the area? This is definitely something you want to know.

Heating, Ventilation, Air Conditioning

Sources of heating, air conditioning, and ventilation can be important when collecting information on a target. The location of these sources as well as how they are powered may be useful. Determining the amount and frequency of noise generated by the machines providing these services can be of benefit in masking any noise you may make when you have to move in the area.

Communications

When conducting a rural surveillance operation on individuals or facilities, information concerning communications is one of the highest priorities. Knowing the target's communications capabilities or the lack of them can be of vital importance. This is a capability you and the team need to determine as soon as possible, as an active communications capability can be a real threat to your team and the surveillance operation. In addition to determining if there is telephone service—either landline or cell-phone capability—you should look for any handheld radios or antennas that may be used.

Security

Whether the security is well organized and well armed or just some alert individuals, any security measures in the target area can pose a threat to you and your surveillance mission. If there is a security consciousness at the target, you must be extremely cautious. On a large target with organized security it is best to observe the security in general, outside security, and inside security. This list will help you organize the information you need to collect on security.

- Personnel: How many security personnel are there and do they appear to be alert?
- Weapons: Types; condition; are they loaded?
- Equipment: Handcuffs; flashlights; any other types of equipment?
- Dress/uniforms: Patches; nametags; rank or other insignia?

- Communications: Radios; telephones; frequencies?
- Animals: Are there any animals that are used by or may alert security?
- Cameras: Location; fixed; moving; blind spots?
- Alarm systems: Type; power source?
- Lighting: Locations; power source; illumination; time used?
- Sensors: Type; locations; what are they used to protect?
- Posts: Locations; types; when are they used and how are they are equipped?
- Patrol Areas/routes/schedules: Also include areas that aren't patrolled.
- Outside security: Patrols; posts; shifts; vehicles; alertness; vulnerabilities?
- Inside security: Locations; communications; schedules; rotations?

Medical Concerns

There are two aspects to medical information you should include in your report about the target. The first is concerning any medical capabilities there may be at the target itself. Are there first-aid kits, perhaps in the security building or the main structure? Also, if the target is in a remote area, is there an area nearby or at the target that could be used as a medical evacuation site by rescue helicopters? How long would it take for an ambulance to reach the target area in an emergency? What are the activities in the area that could possibly cause a medical emergency? Is there any indication that there is any medical capability or equipment at the target?

Transportation

The transportation used at the target can often reveal a great deal about the activities and capabilities of the target. Transportation may also indicate the threat. For example, if the only transportation entering and leaving the target area consists of regular cars, then there isn't the same threat as there would be if personnel at the site were riding around in four-wheel drive trucks or all-terrain vehicles. If there are armed security personnel riding through the area on trail bikes, the surveillance team is definitely going to have to consider them a direct threat. If there are horse trails and

evidence that they are being used, be sure to report that information.

Recording Information

Sketching

Accurately sketching an area or a building is difficult enough under favorable conditions; trying to do it in a hide site, with poor lighting and bad weather conditions, is extremely difficult. However, it is something you must do while conducting surveillance. Many people try to memorize the target and sketch it later, but this simply does not work. One of the added benefits of sketching while in a hide site is that it causes you to look at the target more closely and capture more accurate information. Sketching the target and the surrounding area is an excellent aid that helps you to become very familiar with the target in a relatively short period. It's important to sketch the target even if you have been able to get good photographs or video.

With all sketches and photographs, be sure to orient to magnetic north to avoid any confusion later. As you diagram a building or sketch the area you are observing, take a compass reading and orient everything you observe to magnetic north. This way there is no confusion over the direction buildings are facing or the way a subject entered or left the area. It is also important to make a detailed note showing your hide site(s) in relation to the target. (If you see areas that might serve as good hide sites for future operations, it is important to add those to your sketch of the area.)

Don't let your carefully recorded data get destroyed by rain or damp. There is paper designed to be used in a damp environment that can be written on and won't run or smudge. You should *never* use an ink pen to sketch or make your notes because just a small amount of water can ruin them. Always take several small, sharpened pencils to sketch with. Mechanical pencils are fine, but if you decide to use one, be sure to have regular pencils as backups in case the mechanical pencil breaks. Take a small pocketknife to sharpen the pencils if necessary (taking care to pack out any shavings). Also, be sure to use some type of waterproof container to keep your notes and sketches in.

Recording devices such as still and video cameras can be an asset on any collection mission. They can also be a burden if not used properly and protected from the elements. Always use a backup; don't depend too much on electrical devices.

Photographs and Videos

Video cameras can greatly aid a rural surveillance team. Whether you prefer to use a video camera (analog or digital) or a compact digital still camera, these devices can often help to observe or confirm information you may have missed. They also are great for briefing your operation and are very helpful if you are conducting raid planning as a result of your surveillance operation. There are, however, some serious drawbacks you must consider before deciding to use a camera. You will be operating in environments where there is dirt, dust, and damp. With both still and video cameras these and other elements are likely to cause a malfunction that you may not be aware of until you have returned from the operation. Photos and videos of targets are great and are extremely useful in collecting evidence and raid planning, but you can come to rely on them too much. Don't make the mistake of counting on

cameras without backing up your collected information with handmade sketches.

There is nothing quite as good as a photograph sometimes when you want to identify or confirm the identity of a suspect or capture an event. Your rural surveillance mission may be to record activities over an extended period and a 35mm camera may be more practical than a video camera. If you determine that you will be taking a series of photographs over time, it is critical that you keep a photo log that lists details for each picture taken. At a minimum this log should include the time, date, location, circumstances, subject, and photographer for the picture taken. Lighting conditions and weather could also be included. Your photo log, just as the surveillance log, should be consistent in case it is challenged in court.

Covert photography is difficult under the best conditions. If you are going to photograph the target and its activities, and I strongly recommend that you do, practice taking covert pictures before you actually go on an operation to see how difficult it is. Be very aware of how much noise your camera makes when taking a picture and when rewinding film. Don't assume your practice shots came out all right. Have them developed and see if they are good enough to use. This should be incorporated into your team training and practiced. Just as you might train with weapons, camouflage, and equipment, you must also train in how your team collects and records the information you are working so hard to collect.

Chronicling

As you are sketching the target and the target area, taking photographs, or recording video information, you will also need to log the activities that are taking place in and around the target. The most common procedure is to have a standardized format that allows activities to be recorded in chronological order using the 24-hour-clock employed by the military. All activities observed should be recorded; team members need to be trained to record every activity that relates to the target. Even activities that may appear insignificant should be recorded if they take place in the target area, as they may later prove to be of major significance.

By recording all activities in chronological order, information observed by one team can be verified by other teams observing the same target or area. If an extended surveillance operation is being conducted and teams are relieving each other, this allows for uninterrupted surveillance. Using a standardized format also aids the task of consolidating information over time. It is imperative that team members coming off surveillance returns the information they have collected to be reviewed for accuracy and completeness. The information they collect should be reviewed, analyzed, and compiled into a master surveillance record.

While the last thing anyone coming back from surveillance is going to want to do is work on a log, it must be done. If the surveillance operation leads to an operation or raid against the target or if there is going to be a court case, one of the things a lawyer for the defense will attack is how the surveillance was conducted and how information was recorded. By consolidating the information of each phase of the surveillance in a logical and standardized manner, you can minimize challenges to the information you collected.

Specific Target Information

In addition to collecting information on the target area is critical to gather as much specific information as possible. The more specific, the better. Below are lists of items to help you capture detailed information regarding particularly important items you will likely observe in and around the target.

Personnel
- Physical descriptions
- Clothing
- Jewelry
- Habits
- Associates and companions
- Distinguishing characteristics (e.g., scars, tattoos)
- Demeanor (e.g., attitudes, actions, and interactions with others)

Structures
- Type
- Size
- Location
- Doors
- Windows
- Vents
- Heating and cooling
- Roof
- Basement
- Lighting
- Locks
- Vegetation

Vehicles
- Type
- Make
- Model
- Color(s)
- License
- Vehicle identification number (VIN)[1]
- Modifications
- Dents and scratches

- Tires
- Stickers, decals, trim, detailing
- Parking permits (name, color, numbers)
- Membership passes
- Antennas
- Rusting and holes

Weapons
- Types
- Models
- Number
- Condition
- Scopes
- Lasers
- Holsters
- Slings
- Ammunition

Note

1. Yes, it is possible to record something as small as the VIN on a car. Once, some other team members and I moved into the target when the subjects were sleeping because we felt the information we wanted was worth the risk. We went in close to get more than just VINs, but that was part of what was collected. I have also seen team members get VIN numbers with binoculars because they were positioned above an area where vehicles had to stop for traffic. It can be done, but it is hit and miss and very risky. If a team is investigating a car theft ring or believes the suspects are changing plates on vehicles, this is going to be a priority.

Chapter Ten: Mission Completion

At some point you and your team will have successfully collected your information. Many teams make the mistake of becoming too confident at this stage, getting impatient and believing they can start taking shortcuts. Don't make this potentially deadly mistake.

Just because you got into the target area undetected and successfully collected information on a target without being seen doesn't mean the danger is over. All the hard work you and the team have done may be wasted if your operation is compromised, even if it happens after you leave the area.

Leaving undetected also means leaving no sign that you were in the area, which is difficult to do. Every time you enter a remote area you leave some sign that you have been there, and the longer you stay, the greater the chances of dropping something or altering the terrain. Depending on factors such as terrain, vegetation, and weather, you may not be able to leave an area without some indications that you were there. But you must make every effort to eliminate or cover the obvious signs that you were in the area. First and foremost you must check the surveillance hide sites carefully to ensure that nothing is left behind to indicate a human presence. Although individuals or a team may have occupied a hide site for days, it must be completely sanitized before they leave. The best and easiest way to do this is to continually inspect it while it is occupied. One effective method I have seen is to check it each time a team is relieved. The site is then examined to confirm that the departing individual or group has left nothing.

In one British surveillance school where these operations are taught, if a student or team of students leaves any sign that a human has occupied a hide site, they fail the course. Some may think this is an extreme measure, but when you realize that these demanding standards save lives and ensure mission success, it becomes understandable. On one occasion, a two-man team left a hide site they had occupied for less than 24 hours. When asked if they had completely sanitized their hide site they gave assurances that they had. After they were gone, an instructor inspected their site and found a very small scrap of paper and a lead point that had broken off one of their pencils. They didn't graduate. Following that incident no sites were left with any signs that could be attributed to human beings. You must leave any hide site or base camp you occupy totally sterile.

GETTING OUT

Just as you employed stealth, camouflage, concealment, noise, and light discipline to tactically move into an area, you must also do the same when leaving. Just because you believe that you have not been detected during the operation doesn't mean that you will remain so. I believe that the time between ending the surveillance and safely returning to a secure area away from the target is one of the most dangerous and vulnerable times of the entire surveillance operation, because when you and your team pack up and start moving away from the target there is a natural tendency to let your guard down. Either consciously or subconsciously, people will begin to feel that the mission is over and all they need to do is walk away to their pickup point. Also, team members are usually tired and hungry and all they can think about is getting home, cleaning up, getting some food, and resting. I understand it and have felt that way many times myself.

I recall being with a group of deputies that had just completed a 3-day operation and all they wanted to do was get in the pickup vehicle and get home. They felt they had done a good job and that since they were several kilometers away from the target at the pickup point they could relax. They were feeling confident even though they were still in the operational area and weren't that far away from the target. One individual was so excited about being finished that he was relaxing on the ground and casually talking in a normal voice to others in the group. To make matters worse, as they were waiting for their pickup, they had failed to put out any security and had made little effort to ensure they weren't being followed. Fortunately for the team no one was tracking them, but if someone had wanted to walk up on them it would have been very easy. What had been a reasonably successful mission could have quickly turned into a disaster simply because they let their guard down before the mission was over. Remember that any time you are in the operational area, the mission is not over until you have safely returned home. And even then it isn't completely over.

Whenever possible, the location you select for your team to be picked up should be different from the one where you entered the area and made your way to the target. There are good tactical reasons for this. One of the most important reasons is that if your entry or drop-off point was observed it must be considered compromised. Someone may assume you will be leaving from the same area you came in and could be waiting for you to return. If your entry was detected someone could also have followed your tracks and might be waiting at any point along the way

you took to your target. Whenever possible, select an extraction or pickup point well away from the location your team was dropped off when you began your surveillance operation. It's good tactics.

The best time to have your team picked up is during the hours of darkness when there is little or no civilian traffic or activity in the area. Even if it means waiting several hours until activities in the area settle down, do it. Remember the team is most vulnerable when it is being dropped off or being picked up from an operation.

Just as you did during the drop-off of the team at the beginning of the operation, be sure to have contingencies for any threats or problems you encounter. Make sure all team members know what to do if they are detected or if there is an injury or any other problems that come up before or during the pickup. Also, establish rallying points for use in an emergency.

DEBRIEFING THE TEAM

Each time a team member or members come away from the target, they should be debriefed as soon as it is practical to do so. How you do it and who is primarily responsible is not as important as the fact that you conduct a debriefing and that it is thorough and consistent.

PRESENTING YOUR INFORMATION

Whether your rural surveillance operation was for a few hours or lasted much longer, you will have a great deal of information that needs to be organized and given in a logical and professional manner at a briefing. You may not realize it at first, but any time you conduct a good surveillance operation you will observe and collect a great deal of useful information. I never cease to be amazed when I observe an operational briefing given as though it was a bull session discussing a sporting event. Not only is it unprofessional, it diminishes those who are participating. It also sends a message

Conduct a thorough debriefing of the entire team as soon as you possibly can.

to others that you are less than professional and don't take the subject as seriously as you should. Don't let this happen to you. If you have worked hard on surveillance of a target and put yourself at risk, make the effort to give a thorough and professional briefing. In so doing, you will likely be assigned more surveillance missions.

If your surveillance operation lasts for an extended time and produces a lot of data, you should start organizing the information and planning your briefing while still in the field. If you don't, you may have trouble organizing your briefing when you return. Some prefer to present only those things that took place on the target while others describe their operation from the time they deployed to the time they returned. The important thing is to present the information so as to provide a clear picture of what took place on the target and determine if the objectives of the mission were accomplished. It's a good idea to state exactly what your objectives were at the beginning of the briefing. This establishes the reason for the

briefing and is a good starting point for getting everyone on the same page.

Whatever point you decide to begin your briefing from, take those you are briefing through the operation in chronological order. In so doing, you will be able to give them a clear picture of what the team did and what they observed. Your briefing should be detailed to the point that those receiving it can see in their mind the activities you and your team saw while conducting the surveillance. As a result, those you brief will be better able to absorb the information the surveillance provides and will have an appreciation for what your team can do and what it went through to collect the information.

I would caution you to use good security practices when conducting a briefing on an operation even though the operation has been completed. You never know when you may have to return to the same area, so the fewer people who know you were ever there, the better. Whenever possible, do not reveal your team's operational procedures and tactical techniques.

These are skills that need to remain among the members of the team and could cause a mission to fail if they were compromised. The fact that you have such a capability needs to be protected as much as possible.

Any time you can provide photos, videos, and sketches of the target, do so. Not only will it greatly improve your briefing; it will also go a long way in demonstrating the value and professionalism of your team's capabilities. This being said, you should never take undue risks on the operation just to have extra materials for a briefing. I've seen this done, and the risk far exceeds the gain. A thorough, professionally delivered briefing can go a long way to ensure command-level support for your team and can help to win a case if it goes to trial.

Lessons Learned

Conducting a lessons-learned session can be a real education even for the most experienced operators. It is a real eye-opener for people who have never been involved in a session focused on addressing everything that took place and finding resolution for problems, or perceived problems, that occurred on the operation. Lessons learned should also be a part of every training session a rural surveillance team conducts, whether the training takes place in the field or a classroom. Many people believe that the only time to do a lessons-learned session is when the operation or the training is over. Actually, you should constantly be doing it.

I trained a SWAT team recently, and we were working on tactical movement at night. It was really a great team of dedicated professionals, but it was immediately obvious to me and to them that they needed a lot of work. Within the first several hundred meters we had to stop and totally reorganize their procedures to correct several mistakes. They were not moving in a tactical formation and were not prepared to move as a team in the dark; they did not give their eyes time to adjust to the increased darkness created by the dense foliage; and they did not have themselves organized as to who was supposed to be in what position.

They simply thought they could start walking into the woods and not plan their movement.

After several adjustments and a long night, they were really looking like a different team and the adjustments they made did the trick. Their team leader was outstanding, and for the remainder of the week of training they constantly were conducting lessons-learned sessions and made a number of needed adjustments. As a result, they left the training a much better team with increased capabilities and higher team morale.

Conducting professional, direct lessons-learned sessions can go a long way toward improving team morale. I have been in lessons-learned sessions where team members have said some very direct things about what they believed to be operational problems and others took offense. There is always the potential for this to happen and it is not always a bad thing. As long as it doesn't get personal and the problem is addressed and solved, the "tell it like it is" approach can be a good thing. However, it is up to the team leaders to ensure the sessions remain focused and do not become a "bitch session" or an attack on individuals.

These sessions need to have focus and organization. If they don't, the team members can get off track and never get around to addressing areas that need attention. Whether you organize the meeting to address specific subjects or address events that took place, keep it organized and have someone in charge to keep the meeting moving and on track. It is important to have someone recording issues and problems raised during the discussions so the team can refer to this record later. One extremely important aspect of the lessons-learned sessions that is often overlooked is assigning a *specific* person to take the corrective action and report back on the status of the issue. The actions to be taken and who is responsible should be included in the records of the meeting. A team that consistently conducts lessons-learned reviews can only improve. It is one of the best ways I know of for a team to learn from its mistakes and experiences.

This process doesn't have to be complicated; often the simpler approach is better. Whenever you conduct a lessons-learned session, include any support personnel who were involved in the operation; you may want to have a separate session with them. Just some basic questions may be all you need to get the information.

What worked well? What didn't?

What problems did we have and how do we fix them?

What could we have done better?

MAINTAINING MISSION INFORMATION

Once an operation is completed and the briefing is over, the information collected and presented should be securely stored. Likewise, the information gained at the debriefing should be securely stored. Some teams have been known to take their briefing notes, sketches, photos, and everything else and throw them away. They reason that the job is finished and they won't ever need it again, only to discover weeks or months later that they are going back to the same target. The next time there may be new members on the team who could benefit from the information collected on the previous operation. DO NOT throw away any information you collect on an operational target.

Even if your team conducts training in an area, save any maps or sketches of the area when the training is finished.

However, if you have duplicates of sketches, operational notes, photographs, or anything else that provides information about your operation, make sure they are destroyed. You don't want anything about your training or operations left unsecured. Also, ensure that no one can access any remaining information without the team leader's permission.

FOLLOW-UP TRAINING

The difference between a great rural surveillance team and an average or mediocre team is how much it trains together and how hard it works to improve its capabilities and professionalism. The best way to train your team is to exercise against a training target just as you would plan and operate against an actual one. As with any training, there are limitations and restrictions you have to work with but you can get around these with some effort. Since it may be difficult to find time for a rural surveillance team to train together, it is important to make the most of the time you have. It will also be important to make the training as realistic as possible. When I train teams, the training almost always incorporates every phase of a rural surveillance operation, from beginning to end.

The best way I have found to train teams is to give them a scenario against a target and let them work against that target as though they were going after the real thing. To make it as realistic as possible, I recommend that you select a target that is typical of the kind of targets your team is most likely to encounter in a real situation. The target you use should be challenging to the team and should be one that team members are not familiar with. I prefer to have the target occupied with some activity in and around the area. This makes the operation more challenging and will prevent the team members from becoming bored and complacent. However, there is also training value to having the team focusing on a target where there is no activity and the exercise results in there being nothing to report. Dealing with boredom is something a team needs to learn.

When I train a team and we are working against a target, most of the time I employ targets where there has been no coordination. By this I mean that neither the occupants of the target nor the local law enforcement agencies have been contacted. When I do coordinate with the occupants, after receiving their permission I let them know the time frame of the training operation. I usually ask them to do some things and to refrain from others. If you use this technique, use your own imagination about what activities the target will engage in to make the exercise more interesting and challenging for the team. You need to make sure it is controlled and that if you ask for this participation, those you use will keep it to themselves at least during the conduct of the exercise. Once the training is completed, determine if the people supporting the exercise observed or heard anything that might have led to compromising a real operation.

When I use people on the target, I like to ask them to actually look for the team periodically. I don't let the team know from exercise to exercise whether this is going to happen or if any activity is coordinated. This adds realism to the training and the team treats it as the challenge that it is. It can quickly become a contest, and your team will participate in the exercise much more enthusiastically. Whether it is an assistant instructor or the residents of the target, it is a good idea to have someone actually looking for the team during a portion of the training. This is especially effective at night if someone occasionally shines a light out in the area to see if they can observe anything. But you don't want it to get out of control, where someone gets so involved that he disrupts the training and it becomes counterproductive; this is always a possibility, so you need to be very selective when using outside assistance.

Make sure that the scenarios you use are realistic so the team will take them seriously. Also, mix them up so the team learns to be prepared for different types of situations. Have an exercise scenario starting out as a surveillance on a drug house that turns into a raid and incorporates a changing situation. This is a great way to keep the team prepared. I know of one department that is so committed to having a well-trained team that it periodically calls them out for a training exercise that the team in fact believes is an actual operation. This team enjoys the full support of the sheriff and the command staff. This has paid off many times for them in the success of their actual operations. Probably no other departments in the country today are as capable of knowing what is going on in their jurisdictions or able to quickly and discreetly find out as is this department. I wish every department in America had this type of

commitment. Because of the realistic and aggressive training and support the team receives, it is a motivator for other officers to work to a higher level to become members of this team.

Another effective way to train your team is to divide the team and have one half set up in an area and have the other half of the team looking for it. This is excellent training for the hunters and the hunted. But this is also the type of training that must be very controlled with established rules and constraints. On one occasion I was training a class that was made up of three different teams. One team would move into an area and set up observation points, and another team would have to move through the area in an attempt to spot those in hiding. The teams then reversed roles and either hid or searched for the other. It led to some excellent training, and all the team members learned very quickly about some things they were doing right and problems they needed to correct.

One other suggestion concerning training is to use it as a vehicle to build leadership in all the members. You never know when the team leader or anyone else is going to be on vacation, sick, or injured. Every person on a rural surveillance team needs to be trained in the duties of other members of the team. The best method of developing and ensuring this capability is to give people the opportunity to do someone else's job.

If you have an exercise coming up, once the team is assembled give the situation and mission to the group and then turn command over to one of the less experienced team members. It's up to you whether you allow him to run the entire operation or just handle it for the first few hours. You may want him to handle the planning and briefing and then take back control. You may decide to turn to someone else who needs training in leadership and tell him that he is now in charge. This is an excellent way to build leadership skills in your team and it also provides an understanding and appreciation for how difficult the job is and why things are done a certain way. The U.S.

military has used this method for building leaders and training its people for decades, and it is a great way to instill leadership. Also, when other members of the team know they will find themselves in this role at some time, they are much more likely to get behind the person who is temporarily in charge and support making the mission a success.

Nothing beats good, realistic training. Not only does training help to keep your team sharp and capable, good training is a great morale booster. It's great for team-building and camaraderie. Most important, it increases the likelihood of success and can save lives. Get your team out as often as possible and give it the training it needs. Having the support of your department or supervisor is critical. Insist on equipping and training your rural surveillance team so it can do the job safely and correctly. The information a well-trained and properly employed rural surveillance operation can produce is truly worth it.

About the Author

Van Ritch served 22 years in the U.S. Army, but his career did not take the normal career path. Serving as a Special Forces officer and as a counterintelligence agent, he had a number of interesting assignments as well as some unique "training opportunities." One of the more interesting and challenging of these was with the British Army's Special Intelligence Operations course, in which a wide variety of surveillance techniques were taught. These techniques have been used successfully in Northern Ireland and throughout the world to collect sensitive intelligence and to support special operations and counterterrorist operations.

While serving in West Berlin as the officer in charge of counterespionage for the U.S. sector, he witnessed at firsthand the value of surveillance both as a valuable tool for collecting information and a defensive measure for protecting yourself, your fellow team members, and your sources. He learned the value of being able to use the terrain—both urban and natural—to assist with surveillance of the "bad guys." While most investigators were content to conduct surveillance from the comfort of their vehicles, Ritch and a few of the bolder agents learned to blend into the surrounding areas and were able to ensure successful surveillance operations.

Following the 3-year tour in Berlin, Ritch was invited to attend the U.S. Army Special Forces course. After successfully completing training, he was assigned to the 7th Special Forces Group at Fort Bragg, North Carolina. During his tour with the 7th Group Ritch

served first as the counterintelligence officer, where he developed an urban operations course designed to train Special Forces teams to operate and survive in a hostile urban environment. He later commanded a Special Forces "A" team whose primary mission was training for counterterrorist operations. This team was also periodically tasked to conduct penetration operations against sensitive government facilities to determine their security vulnerabilities.

After his tour as an "A" team commander, Ritch was hand-picked by Col. Nick Rowe to develop the U.S. Army's SERE (Survival, Evasion, Resistance, and Escape) school. In this capacity, he served as operations officer and supervised the development and delivery of course instruction. During this assignment, Ritch and selected NCOs also developed evasion routes and procedures for U.S. military personnel operating in Honduras. It was also during this time that the SERE committee developed the U.S. Army's antiterrorist and personnel protection course for at-risk personnel serving or traveling overseas into high-threat areas.

Ritch was later assigned to a special operations unit where he conducted intelligence duties and trained friendly foreign military personnel in special operations and intelligence techniques. Following several other special operations and intelligence assignments, several of which were of a classified nature, Ritch decided to retired from the army.

After his army career, he began training law enforcement officers at the North Carolina Justice Academy. Initially Ritch was asked to oversee the academy's flagship course, which was designed to train law enforcement leaders in managing and leading their agencies. It was during this time that a number of hostage incidents were taking place throughout the United States and that a bomb was planted at the 1996 Olympics in Atlanta, Georgia. The main suspect, Eric Rudolph, was skilled in backwoods survival techniques and was thought to be hiding in the wilderness. Visiting the field headquarters site in western North Carolina where the FBI, ATF, and other state and local agencies had set up headquarters, Ritch quickly determined that operating in rural areas was one enforcement capability that these police agencies just did not possess. In talking to other agency representatives, he realized that a course needed to be developed to train law enforcement officers to operate in a rugged rural environment. What began as a 1-week course quickly turned into a very intensive 3-week training course with the same subject areas as in this book. The course consisted of many practical exercises and hands-on training experiences.

Ritch saw that this unique and valuable training was needed by law enforcement agencies throughout the nation. Combining this course with his training and experiences serving with special operations units, Ritch has developed a course of training for U.S. law enforcement agencies. Today he conducts this training for selected individuals and agencies throughout the country.